FACING ETERNITY

FACING ETERNITY

How to Know Where You Will Go When You Die

by
Willard A. Ramsey

MILLENNIUM III PUBLISHERS
Simpsonville, South Carolina
1999

Millennium III Publishers
PO Box 928
Simpsonville, SC 29681

ISBN 0-9625220-4-X

To Robyn, Prudence, and Shaun — our faithful three — who anticipate eternity with delight.

CONTENTS

FOREWORD

This book removes masks. How uncomfortable —
but how many faces lie beneath!

Facing Eternity begins by breaking down the contemporary masks of ignorance against the Almighty God
and His eternal truths. This book has the tenacity to
face down the seeming fixity of modern ideas and words
we hold over our eyes, trying not to see God seeing our
guilt before His law, trying not to see ourselves seeing
the desperation with which we don the masks of
blindmen.

But when the mask is off, what will the sinner see?
What will the Christian present to the seeking eyes of
an asking soul? Let it be truth! Let it be the full truth
about himself and his God. This book would show the
sinner his lawlessness, his peril, his dependence on a
God who expresses love, anger, compassion, wisdom.
This book would face the realities of eternity alongside
the seeking sinner, pointing out to him the landscape of
that awesome vastness. It gives a clear-eyed look at the
blackness of hell, radiance of heaven.

This book seeks to be a faithful companion to those
it unmasks, a friend to those unbelievers who would first
squint, rheumy eyes dazzled, at the scope of the real.
This book would rather be true to the sinner's eternal
needs than dupe to the sinner's momentary comfort. In
this Willard Ramsey shows himself a friend indeed: by
wounding faithfully rather than kissing deceitfully. He
refuses to veil the Gospel.

Too many Christians have shown themselves easy

and false friends to the sinner. Let it not be so — may we repent and learn better ways, even from this book. We do no good when we drone the saccharine monotone of Christ as mere Caregiver, or give the timorous ping of Gospel as mere formula. We can do better: we can sound forth the riches of a full and realistic Gospel, and things will change when we do. And we will ourselves be awed when we face anew the might of God's Law, the *depth* of His Love (a love which has no shallow). And we will attain boldness — boldness to unmask a hiding world fierce in its cowardice.

It is in the face of the Gospel unveiled that we see the ways of a Lord whose face is, indeed, set against them who do evil, but who is near the contrite. These contrite He teaches through the words of His servants — even, by His grace, through this little book.

Facing Eternity is an unusual book — though I look forward to a day when it will be lost in a crowd of others like it — unusual because it neither masks nor trivializes its Gospel cargo. It is the work of a seasoned Christian facing eternity with steady, seeing eyes.

May God prosper this book.

DEREK ALEXANDER
St. John's College, Annapolis
December, 1998

PREFACE

The massive influence of naturalistic and pluralistic philosophies, in recent decades, has essentially dissipated the last remnants of the fading traditional Christian heritage and worldview from our culture. In this book we have shown that these modern and postmodern philosophies are intellectually barren and morally corrosive, but nevertheless, they have stealthily overtaken the masses of our culture without their knowledge, leaving them not only without hope but with no hope of hope.

The Gospel, therefore, falls on deaf ears. In a desperate effort to get crowds, many churches have adopted a strategy of accommodation and appeasement; but their evangelism is powerless and off message.

This book exemplifies a different strategy. Like missionaries to a pagan country, we must assume that little or no Christian background remains in our culture. Evangelism must reestablish the concept of God as a transcendent, personal, rational Creator. We must redefine the basics: 1) God's law as with penalty, 2) divine retribution, 3) the legal jeopardy of the sinner; 4) Christ as Lord, and His death as legal satisfaction for sin, 5) regeneration, with repentance and faith as the immediate duty of every sinner, and 6) the fruits of repentance in the Christian life.

This is a major paradigm shift — back to the evangelistic emphases of the Great Awakenings. Will it bring the same result today? We believe it will if enough pastors and evangelists have the courage and wisdom to make the shift.

CHAPTER 1

Orientation: The Bleak Outlook For the Unbeliever

Out there somewhere are those who are searching for the help this book offers. You have thought about your future beyond college, beyond your career, beyond retirement, and beyond the grave. You are wise enough to know that you may face eternity before you have lived out your normal life span. You may die young, or you may die old and full of years. But you know you will die.

So you also need to know the God who transcends all these things — all life, all sorrow, and all death. He has His eye on you who seek Him, and He thinks about you. "For I know the thoughts that I think toward you, says the LORD, thoughts of peace and not of evil, to give you a future and a hope" (Jer. 29:11, NKJV). The future is in God's hands; therefore eternity is slanted toward good because God is good. His mercy, to those who seek Him, endures forever.

Before you can know this God, however, there are some hurdles to clear. There will be issues to face that you won't like. But you'll face them. You'll see them for the chains of bondage they are. At first, like all who have gone before you, there'll be some dread and trepidation. Just as a person with a serious illness dreads a doctor's diagnosis, so we dread God's diagnosis of our sins. But you'll focus on the cure and refuse to be paralyzed by the dread.

The first and oldest problem felt as an effect of sin was the dread to approach God and to learn the real truth of our status before Him. It is a fear of knowing the truth, but it won't stop you because you *seek* the truth.

In the first chapter we will consider the downward course of sustained unbelief when it is followed to its logical conclusion. In the last four chapters, we will consider the truths comprising the rock-solid foundation of the eternal hope of the believer.

Gnostiphobia

The *first* and most basic problem to consider is this ancient dread of facing the truth about God. *Gnostiphobia* means a *fear of knowing*. Every year many people die needlessly because they are unwilling to face the reality of disease and death until it's too late. They are *gnostiphobic,* afraid to *know* the truth about their physical condition, when the cure is often easily available. In the spiritual realm there is an almost exact parallel except that gnostiphobia is a thousand-fold more common toward the truth about God, sin, and eternal destinies than about medical matters.

Gnostiphobia was the very first human reaction toward God after the first sin. The first thing Adam and Eve did after their disobedience was to hide from God. "I heard thy voice in the garden, *and I was afraid . . ."* Dressing themselves in fig leaves, they dreaded any contact with Him. This fear of the knowledge of God is no new problem. This is not a sideline issue. It is probably the number one reason why people go out into eternity unprepared to meet God. It is a basic feature of the non-Christian disposition.

Millions of people are just plain uncomfortable with subjects like God, Jesus Christ, sin, salvation, heaven, hell. They do not necessarily deny them but neither do they accept them. The discomfort level is just too high to consider the matter seriously. They do not *deny;* they are *in denial.*

This can be true of religious people, even of many with traditional Christian backgrounds. Many church members simply go through the motions, having immunized themselves against the message or rationalized their behavior pattern.

There are many reasons why people react negatively to issues of God's righteousness and truth. First, God's truth implies the necessity of change, and change is uncomfortable. Ignorance is comfortable; it protects our traditions, our pride, and our sins. Sin loves the shelter of darkness. That's why establishments featuring immoral activities are usually dimly lit; "... men loved darkness rather than light, because their deeds were evil" (John 3:19).

It has long been said that "ignorance is bliss." This point is expressed really well by Melanie McKinstry in an unpublished monograph entitled "The Encyclopedia of Ignorance." She wrote:

> Man wants to remain in the dark for the security, the warmth, the stability. In the dark, man's pride remains unchallenged, his intelligence isn't all shot . . . . When

man is forced into the light, he may have to question everything he has been taught. He may have to question everything *mama* told him to believe. In Socrates' "Allegory of the Cave," man, no matter what his situation, may choose to stay in the dark if it means saving his pride, his beliefs, his comfort. He does not care if it is wrong. He chooses to embrace his ignorance — even if it means blowing out the only candle in his dungeon. For in the dark he cannot see the truth walking towards him with a dagger.

The anxiety about facing God can be deadly. If there is truth behind subjects like God, Christ, sin, heaven, hell; the eternal implications which attach to these issues would make our knowledge of and positive response to them to be the highest order of priority. Were we created by an all-powerful God? Is there a hell? Is Jesus Christ the only Savior? Before we can possibly know if these issues may be safely dismissed, we must consider them. It would be a serious mistake to let the fear of knowing prevent you from even giving these basic questions of life a serious hearing.

In this case, what you don't know *can* hurt you. Where eternal destinies are at stake, accurate knowledge is critical. If unchangeable absolute truths do exist, by the nature of the case they are urgent matters calling for immediate attention.

Jesus said, "Seek and you will find." Others say there are no objective absolute truths to find. But then unless you seek you'd never know — until it's too late — would you? Many solve the anxiety problem by rationalizing and ignoring the issues. Others solve the anxiety problem more safely. They face it. They seek the truth and find it.

When one resolves in his or her heart to seek the

Lord, when one faces up to the issue and comes truly to know Him, he or she finds there is nothing to dread and everything to love in the full knowledge of His truth. To know Him is to love Him.

Gnostiphobia and Our Pluralistic Society

Now a *second* downward step of sustained unbelief, on the way to its logical conclusion, leads to yet a more serious development. As anti-Christian doctrines come and go, they each seem designed to ease or relieve the ancient problem of gnostiphobia. Remember the first defense against the fear of confronting God was fig leaves, but through the centuries more sophisticated theories have been developed — all equally ineffective but having more dangerous side effects. In recent years gnostiphobia has found renewed boldness and comfort in *philosophical pluralism,* a new offensive against God's objective, absolute truths.

Maybe "pluralism" is a new word to you, but millions in recent decades have been affected by it. Numerous ethnic, religious, and political ideologies are growing in America under the influence of pluralism, while the truths of biblical Christianity are more and more being obscured by it.

Unbelievers, in the long-range search for effective ways to avoid God, now appear to have discovered in philosophical pluralism a comfortable new creed which seems to defeat all challenges. This philosophy is so comforting to the gnostiphobic that its true patrons can lie down beside a ticking time bomb and be quite relaxed (until it explodes). This creed has only one article: *the only absolute truth is that there is no absolute truth!*

Virtually everyone, unfortunately, has been affected by it to some degree. Dr. D. A. Carson describes *philosophical pluralism* as a stance:

> . . . that any notion that a particular ideological or religious claim is intrinsically superior to another is *necessarily* wrong. . . . No religion has the right to pronounce itself right or true, and the others false, or even (in the majority view) relatively inferior.[1]

This view so pervades our culture today that all but the most spiritually alert have, to some degree, been subconsciously jaded. The trend to disregard any claim of objective, absolute truth is growing rapidly. Our schools from kindergarten to the university, our entertainment and news media, literature and the arts, governments and legal institutions — our whole culture contributes to this process. In pluralistic thinking there is no room for absolutes, and this provides a deceptive comfort to the basic human dread to face the reality of God.

Human societies throughout history have been seeking a means to minimize the anxiety toward the absolute God. Now, pluralism seems to have found the perfect solution — that there is no objective truth, no absolute standard of right and wrong and therefore no sin, no hell, nor any need for the Gospel of Christ.

The pluralistic philosophy has pervaded all the agents of influence in our society, and through them is undermining all moral and spiritual verities including the Gospel itself. The extent to which this has happened is truly surprising. Carson says:

> . . . modern politics and law trivialize all values, all religious devotion. This stance is now in the air we breathe. The extent to which it has invaded the church is trou-

bling. Not less troubling, for the preacher of the gospel, is the extent to which it is everywhere assumed, especially by middle and upper class, by the media and print elite, by almost all who set the agenda for the nation.

> . . . fully 64 percent strongly agree or agree somewhat with the assertion that "there is no such thing as absolute truth."[2]

These massive influences, coupled with natural human gnostiphobia, leave people today in greater trouble than they know or are willing to admit. A little reflection reveals that if there is an absolute truth or reality behind the universe, the pluralistic creed guarantees that its patrons could never find it.

Since God, by definition, is the absolute, it follows then that the pluralistic creed, which denies all absolutes, is atheistic in nature. Therefore, as long as one holds to it he has, consciously or not, effectively cut himself off from God. For consistency he must retreat to atheism or at least into practical atheism, i.e., to ignore God in life. Unfortunately, this position describes more people than we care to think.

So far the non-Christian stands on very marshy ground that will not support his weight.

Surrender of Absolutes: a Downward Spiral

A *third* downward step of sustained unbelief leads ultimately to moral crises in most individuals and in societies. The dread of knowing our true condition before God has given rise to many rationalizations and self-inflicted blind-spots, including the pluralistic philosophy and the surrender of absolute truth. Closely related is the common notion that this present life is all that there is and that there is nothing beyond the grave.

These notions have grown upon the consciousness of recent generations from youth by constant exposure to an evolutionary worldview. These ideas are void of the concept of a Creator God and of life with Him beyond the grave — another example of a long-standing effort to avoid accountability to God. "Like an old tree," we are led to believe, "we fall and are assimilated into the cosmos."

But what about the fine qualities of vibrant and passionate human spirits — that laughed and loved, cried and sacrificed, defended noble causes, and accomplished valiant deeds? These clearly reflect intelligence, order, and purpose. Are we to believe these are only ethereal echoes of *chance* that vanish finally, as we are told, into nothingness and are no more? Worse yet, are we to be reincarnated perchance as a bug, a frog, or a thief to relive life after miserable life on the way to some vague, ethereal nirvana for which there is no objective eyewitness, as in the case of the Christian heaven (John 6:38; 17:5; Rev. 21:1-22:8)?

These depressing notions are relative late developments, historically speaking, in the Western world. They are sustained by the ever present influence of some theoretical form[3] of evolution[4] driven by chance and the "survival of the fittest."

Chance and survival, as the prime movers or "creators" in this philosophy, have been substituted for a moral Creator God wherever evolution has been popularly taught for an extended period. At the center of the survival motive is the *self*. When our venerable institutions of learning teach that the driving force of life is self survival at the expense of the less fit, the whole social order suffers decadence. Inordinate self-esteem, self-centeredness, violence, crime, immorality, dysfunctional families, and the non-Christian educational and cultural philosophies that feed all of these, are to a great extent the result of over a century of evolutionary indoctrination.

Our children have, by implication at least, been indoctrinated with the philosophy that they themselves are the centerpiece of life because survival of the individual is the driving force of evolutionary progress. Then, when life is over, they look forward only to final extinction.

With that depressing worldview thrust upon children by their teachers and culture, while barring Christian values and hope from the classroom, why wouldn't they throw morality to the winds and grab all the gusto they can? The Apostle Paul shows clear insight into the way hopelessness affects human behavior when he said, ". . . if the dead rise not[,] let us eat and drink; for to morrow we die" (1 Cor. 15:32). Paul's insight has been amply vindicated by the lifestyles of this generation.

This is a bleak picture!

Such hopelessness occurs in both individuals and societies whenever God's absolute truths are abandoned. Hopelessness has fostered the cynical outlook of millions of people today; *and barrenness of soul has engendered decadent behavior ranging from teen suicide, to road rage, to schoolhouse terrorism, to lying and instant sexual gratification in high and low places, to gross indifference of the people, and much, much more!*

Violence and moral chaos in this life, and hell in

the next, is a great price to pay for personal autonomy and insubordination to our Creator God. But the individual does not have to go down with the culture. God changes individuals who seek Him, and individuals change cultures.

The departure of individuals from the creation paradigm, from the law of God, and from the hope of Jesus Christ is at the base of these problems. It is inevitable that unless people abandon the fear of the knowledge of God, this pattern will intensify. Neither a person nor a culture can surrender the spiritual, moral, and eternal verities without a crisis of moral decay; it is only a matter of time. And after that, we meet God.

Surrender of Knowledge: A Shot in the Head

Sustained and persistent unbelief leads to a *fourth* level of descent still more fatal to one's humanity. Where nothing is absolute, nothing can be known. When a person thus negates God, whether to directly reject Him or simply to passively ignore Him, he or she surrenders a priceless gift — credibility as a rational being. This naturalistic human thinking strips its advocate of *knowledge* itself — the one thing that most clearly distinguishes humanity from the rest of creation.

We do not here assert that non-Christians cannot or do not acquire a functional awareness of facts or truth. Of course they do. But as they do, they must use, or rather usurp, Christian presuppositions.

Science and knowledge must proceed upon the assumption that there are consistent principles and uniform laws governing our universe, and that means there are absolutes. Thus when non-Christian naturalistic thinkers are building automobiles or space vehicles, they appeal unwittingly to an orderly Christian universe of uniform laws — not chaotic chance — while ignoring the truth that an orderly universe points to God. But when they consider *origins* and *destinies,* they appeal to an evolutionary process in a chance-driven chaotic universe, having no purpose, no moral basis, no absolutes. Thus in the effort to suppress the knowledge of a Creator God and avoid responsibility to Him, they must forfeit any comprehensive, self-consistent philosophy of being.

Naturalistic man therefore, can *know* nothing standing upon his own assumption

> . . . that time or chance is ultimate. On his assumption his own rationality is a product of chance. On his assumption even the laws of logic which he employs are products of chance. The rationality and purpose that he may be searching for are still bound to be products of chance.[5]

Thus, unless we acknowledge that we are created by and are subordinate to God, we surrender the one valid basis we have upon which to claim rationality.

> It will then appear that Christian theism, which was first rejected because of its supposed authoritarian character, is the only position which gives human reason a field for successful operation and a method of true progress in knowledge[6]

Apart from God none of us would have any basis for rationality or knowledge, because none of the alternatives are based in rational causes. The choices are God or evolution. Evolution is driven by chance, and chance is a random, irrational, chaotic,[7] phenomenon without order or purpose, providing no basis for rationality or knowledge. Therefore, as products of evolution we could never know where we came from or where we are going. In fact we could never *know* anything.

If our brains were the product of impersonal, evolutionary chance, knowledge couldn't exist. Our "thoughts" would be merely a mirage caused by the chance gyrations of senseless molecules dancing randomly without purpose in our heads. One would not be a person but a *process.* How then could such a process *know?* What basis would one have to assert that what this process "sees" or "thinks" is real and reliable? There would be none. Neither would we be thinking about it or asking these questions. If that were the reality of things, *knowledge* wouldn't exist.

In the words of John B. King, Jr., ". . . knowledge is a personal concept which is impossible in the absence of a knowing mind."[8] A computer may solve some very complex problems, but it doesn't *know* it has solved them. After the process, it *indicates* the answer but still doesn't *know* the answer. A computer, though it has an intelligent designer, is only a process, not a person. *Unless we are rational, knowing* spirits — persons — *created by a rational, intelligent God, we have no basis for knowledge, no way to know.*

If, however, we are created persons, living *spirits, designed* as intelligent beings for the *purpose* of receiving intelligence, detecting, analyzing and knowing external realities; and if we are endowed by our Creator with a faculty for rational discernment and understanding, then we can *know.* This leads us to one inevitable conclusion: *All knowledge depends upon the reality that we are spirits created by a rational intelligent designer, the God of the Bible.*[9] We are designed, not by chance, not capriciously, but purposefully, to *know*.

Given our postmodern pluralistic society, we would expect a chorus of voices to take exception to this truth. Someone will surely say, "That philosophy is ridiculous"!

We're sorry, but we have to ask, How do you *know* it is ridiculous? Since you do not acknowledge a rational designer, are you asking us to trust the chaos of chance to produce a rational mind? We don't think so.

We do not mean to sound disrespectful by the starkness of these questions, but it is the clearest way we know to demonstrate the sterility and inconsistency of *denying a rational Creator and then claiming rationality and knowledge.*

If anyone inquires, "Well then, how do *you* know?" The answer is, "We are *designed to know* — all of us"!

Don't deny your birthright! Don't sentence yourself to endless wandering in a murky mirage of midnight darkness, "Ever learning, and never able to come to a knowledge of the truth" (2 Tim. 3:7).

You have then two choices as to the *kind* of God you will believe in: chance, or the God of the Bible! But individual choice does not establish reality; reality has been determined by a power greater than the individual.

If *chance* were your creator, you would never *know* it, because the child of irrational chance is likewise irrational. As previously discussed, knowledge is impossible apart from God, and what we *think* we know is but a dream.

"Well, maybe," some would say, "that's how it is." But don't bet your soul on it.

If chance is the foundation upon which one's belief system rests, it cannot be authenticated. By definition, the phenomenon of chance is inadequate to validate rationality. It can neither impart nor authenticate rationality, intelligence, or knowledge. There is no evidence that would justify a person in believing that chance produces rationality. That is a presuppositional choice, but it is a bad choice because it can never be validated — neither by definition nor by evidence.

That the *God* of the Bible is our Creator is also a presuppositional choice, but it is a good choice because it can be validated: by definition, by revelation, and by evidence.

> For the *wrath of God is revealed from heaven* against all ungodliness and unrighteousness of men, who *suppress the truth in unrighteousness,* because what may be known of God is manifest in them, for God hath shown it to them. For since the creation of the world *His invisible attributes are clearly seen, being understood by the things that are made,* even his eternal power and Godhead; so that they are without excuse (Rom. 1:18-20, NKJV).[10]

Now the presupposition of God as creator is validated by evidence: 1) It is consistent with the biblical definition of God alone, not with chance. Only He can impart rationality, intelligence, order, organized complexity, knowledge. 2) It is validated by God's self-revelation in the entire testimony of the Bible. 3) It is validated by the corroborating evidence of the physical universe so far as it has been tested.

Our reasoning faculties, being also a work of God, are thus authenticated, and the Christian may say, *by faith,* with boldness and convictions that the God of the Bible is absolute reality!

But what is *faith?* Contrary to popular opinion, biblical faith is not a blind leap in the dark. To the contrary, *it is a conviction of truth undergirded by evidence* that is observed and analyzed by the rational, created reasoning power of the mind.

> Now faith is the *substance* (ὑπόστασις, a substructure, basis) of things hoped for, the *evidence* (ἔλεγχος, proof) of things not seen (Heb. 11:1).

Thus the Bible defines *faith* as belief *supported by evidence* — just the opposite of popular opinion, i.e., belief *without* evidence. The "hope" in this passage is the subjective aspect of faith, our belief, confidence, persuasion, or conviction of any matter, but that subjective conviction rests upon a *substructure,* the *proof* of its validity. This evidence or proof that comprises the Christian's faith is derived from two sources:

1) The Scriptures, by far the most complete and reliable source:

> So then *faith cometh* by hearing, and hearing *by the word of God* (Rom. 10:17).

2) The physical universe:

> His invisible attributes *are clearly seen, being understood by the things that are made,* even his eternal power and Godhead (Rom. 1:20).

> The *heavens declare* the glory of God; and the firmament showeth his handiwork. *Day unto day uttereth speech,* and *night unto night showeth knowledge.* There is no speech nor language, where their voice is not heard (Psa. 19:1-3).

Thus, we see in these principles the relationship between presupposition, reason, and faith. *Reason* is the gift of God by which, under the influence of the Holy Spirit, we process the evidence from God's Word (the Bible) and God's works (the physical universe). This evidence, thus assimilated, then becomes a conviction of the heart by *faith* which is the undergirding of our hope of things not seen — our subjective grasp on God's objective truth. Our original *presupposition* is thus validated. But in no part of this whole process does the individual act with complete autonomy, independent of God's superintendency. "For in him we live, and move, and have our being" (Acts 17:28).

The contrary presupposition — that rationality and knowledge may be a product of chance — is refuted 1) by the definition and nature of chance itself, 2) by the revelation of God, the Bible; and 3) by the nature of the physical universe, particularly the laws of entropy, etc. In the face of such contrary evidence and the stark absence of positive evidence such a position could never qualify either as science or faith but is clearly presumptuous. In God's eyes, it has to be sin "for whatsoever is not of faith is sin" (Rom. 14:23), i.e., any belief system not undergirded by evidence is sin.

The naturalistic presupposition, therefore, is best understood as an example of "ungodliness and unrighteousness of men, who suppress the truth in unrighteousness" (Rom. 1:18b, NKJV). Though many are otherwise moral persons, the outlook for the unbeliever is bleak and barren of itself, but worse than that "the wrath of God is revealed from heaven" (1:18a) against all who sustain themselves in unbelief by the suppression of truth.

Unless one presupposes himself to be a product of

the rational God of the Bible, he has no grounds for and no right to demand a place to play in the league of the rational. *He has disqualified himself by his chosen pedigree.* By presupposing[11] himself to be the product of chance, he has relegated himself to the realm of the chaotic and irrational with no place to turn for validation of his thinking processes — having no principle upon which to base rationality.

This is not meant to seem critical or harsh; for all human beings *are* rational, having been created by God, whether acknowledged or not. But those who have been misled by the naturalistic philosophers have denied their birthright, and do not realize what they have done to themselves. *They have not shot themselves in the foot, but in the head.*

In what we believe is a spirit of tough love, R. J. Rushdoony in commending Van Tillian apologetics suggests that Christian witnesses and preachers should

> . . . force the natural man to recognize the meaning of his position, to "tear the mask off the sinner's face" and compel him "to look at himself and the world for what they really are."[12]

If you would draw near to God, you must clear this hurdle — the myth that you can never know the spiritual absolutes about God, origins, Jesus Christ, salvation, and the hereafter. God has revealed these truths to us in the Bible, and has designed us to know, to understand, and to act responsibly toward Him.

> Summing up the whole matter . . . The Christian theistic conception of an absolute God and an absolute Christ and an absolute Scripture go hand in hand. We cannot accept one without accepting the others. . . . All halfway

positions eventually lead to either one or the other of two positions . . . an absolute submission to Scripture and to God or an absolute rejection of both.[13]

We must not sacrifice the eternal spirit given us by the God of absolutes on the altar of the god of chance.

Eternal Verities: Introducing the Absolutes

Now those of you who are sincerely searching for the truth are able to see clearly where a stance of persistent unbelief leads. You can see it is a house built on the sand; intellectually, it is a quagmire offering not even a logical retreat, much less a spiritual sanctuary. But the absolutes of God satisfy ultimately the whole person — body and spirit, intellect and emotions. You are ready now to pursue the positive objective truth of God without looking back and wondering if there is any green grass on the unbeliever's side of the fence. You can now recognize their presuppositions as deceptive chains of bondage.

In the next four chapters we will focus upon Christianity. The religion of the Bible — the religion of Jesus of Nazareth — is about *absolutes*. In stark contrast to the religions of the world, Christianity is about the absolute, truths that guarantee solutions to our most critical *needs*. The religion of Jesus deals with spiritual and eternal verities affecting our lives both in this world and in the hereafter.

Popular religions deal with human self-interest, self-improvement, self-esteem. Their interests focus on incremental change: *longer* life, *better* health, *less* stress, *more* wealth, *improvement, embellishment,* the *temporary — this life.*

The Gospel of Jesus Christ is wholly different. It is not a gospel of mere incremental change in this life only, but a Gospel of quantum change — regeneration by the power of God — into *new* life. Self-interest, self-improvement, and self-esteem are replaced with interests of infinitely greater value. In contrast to popular religions, the objective of God through Christ is not just *longer* life but *eternal* life. God's solutions are not limited to *this life only* but extend to *life after the grave* also.

The Gospel of Jesus Christ is about profound, fundamental change, not change we make in ourselves but change God makes in us. God does not merely *improve* a sinful person; He makes a *new creation* — not merely reformed but *born again, forgiven,* and prepared for *new life* both in this world and in the world to come. God purposes to make us not just morally *better,* but ultimately *perfect;* for in the end He will settle for no less. These are irreconcilable differences between *the absolutes* of Jesus and the shifting sands of popular religions and philosophies that deny absolutes.

We'll all meet God one day, either as a friend or a foe. But if we hope to meet Him as a friend, we must be willing to break the ice, lay aside our gnostiphobic isolation. We must be willing to cut through some temporarily disturbing attitudes and problems, which many people do not even realize they have, before we can reach peace with God.

The rest of this book is about discovering the rock-solid foundations of God's truth that lead to eternal life with its final destiny in the presence of God. That's what all people *need,* even though it may not be what they want in their present state of mind. In fact a person by nature would rather say to God, and to all who speak in His name, "Just leave me alone"!

But you have resolved to seek the truth, and gnostiphobia won't inhibit your search any more. Deep down inside you know God will not leave you alone. "Be still," He said, "and *know* that I am God" (Psa. 46:10).

Having resolved to follow the path of wisdom, you will seek to *know* the truth and focus upon finding the *solution*. A foolish person will continue to be paralyzed by the dread of the problem and die in his or her sins. God has put you where you are today that you may "seek the Lord, if haply [you] might feel after him, and find him, though he be not far from every one of us" (Acts 17:27).

But how does it all work out? Who really is this Lord, you may wonder, that you may make an appeal to Him? These are great questions; and we will discover the answers in the pages to follow.

End Notes:

---

[1]D. A. Carson, *The Gagging of God: Christianity Confronts Pluralism* (Grand Rapids: Zondervan Publishing House, 1996), p. 19. Any one who wants to see a technical and exhaustive analysis and critique of philosophical pluralism will find it in this book, a large tome of 640 pages of first rate scholarship.

[2]Ibid., p. 23.

[3]Evolution is an ancient concept having been held in different forms. Certain ancient Greek philosophies and the Eastern Hindu-based religions include varying concepts of evolution. A quasi-scientific explanation began in the 18th century, maturing with Darwinism in the 19th. Today, certain postmodern concepts go beyond traditional evolution holding the earth itself to be alive — a "grand organism called Gaia" — a New Age pantheistic concept represented by the Gaia Hypothesis. See Dorion Sagan and Lynn Margulis, *Slanted Truths* (New York: Springer-Verlag, 1997), p. 195. Although the Gaia advocates of an autopoietic living biosphere take Neo-Darwinism to task (pp. 280-282), they themselves must hearken back to chance for the origin and evolution of the components of the biosphere.

Sagan and Margulis in *Biospheres from Earth to Space* (Hillsdale, NJ: Enslow Publishers, Inc., 1989) say the "new science" of biospherics has ancient roots: "Our ancestors believed the earth — even the entire universe — to be alive" (p. 86). At bottom, chance-driven evolution remains the only alternative to God in creation. For an informative discussion on Gaia, see Dr. Henry M. Morris, "The Postmodern Agnostics," *Back to Genesis,* July 1998.

[4]The theory of evolution began a rise to popularity in 1859 when Charles Darwin published his book, *On the Origin of Species.* Evolutionary thought has now pervaded the educational systems of the world. But in the last half of the twentieth century a movement of scientists has shown the theory of evolution to be untenable on scientific grounds. There are numerous scientific organizations working in the field of creation science among which are: The **Institute for Creation Research,** P. O. Box 2667, El Cajon, CA 92021; and the **Center for Scientific Creation,** 5612 N. 20th Place, Phoenix, NM 85016. If you want to look into the recent startling developments in creation science, you may write these organizations for a list of their abundant and enlightening publications.

[5]Cornelius Van Til, *The Defense of the Faith* (Phillipsburg, NJ: Presbyterian and Reformed Publishing Co., 1955), p. 102.

[6]Ibid.

[7]By this reference to *chaos* we mean the traditional definition: Confusion; without order, form, purpose, or predictability. We are not referring to Chaos Theory, a mathematical theory dealing with the breakdown of ordered systems, related to fractal geometry, etc. These are not examples of disorder producing order.

[8]John B. King, Jr., "The Creedal Basis of Modern Science: Chalcedon," *Chalcedon Report,* December 1995, p. 15.

[9]If anyone desires to probe deeper into the ironclad philosophical aspects of this idea, we would suggest starting with R. J. Rushdoony, *By What Standard* (Vallecito, CA: Ross House Books, 1995), and then progressing to Cornelius Van Til, *The Defense of the Faith* (Phillipsburg, NJ: Presbyterian and Reformed Publishing Co., 1955). This does not, however, constitute an unqualified recommendation of the full content of these works, valuable as they are.

[10]Italics have been added to many Scripture quotations throughout this book to highlight certain phrases for emphasis or further discussion in the text. All quotations are from the Authorized King James version unless otherwise noted.

[11]Everyone, whether he admits it or not, begins with a presupposition. Carl F. H. Henry has observed there are two kinds of presuppositionalists — those who admit it and those who do not.

[12]R. J. Rushdoony, *By What Standard* (Vallecito, CA: Ross House Books, 1995), p. 106.

[13]Ibid., p. 85, citing Van Til, *Christian Theistic Ethics* (1951), p. 9.

CHAPTER 2

The God Who Creates and Communicates

Millions of people struggle, often for decades, with the really big questions of life. Is there a God? If so, what kind of God is He? Does He know, think, and feel, or is He just an abstract force or influence? What does He want from me? Will I have to appear before Him and give an account of my attitudes and behavior?

We have seen the sterility of the philosophies of the naturalistic unbelievers and have found them false. Now we must search for what is true. We must find the true nature of God and our relationship to Him.

Seek and You Will Find

For those who are sincerely seeking for the truth, it need not be a long struggle. You will find it because you seek for it. Jesus gives us the real secret to knowing God, and that is a true *hungering* to know the real truth no matter what. "Blessed are they which do hunger and thirst after righteousness: for they shall be filled" (Matt. 5:6). Without this, we must forever be in the dark.

If one has no interest in the truth for truth's sake, he will never be motivated to seek for it. Moreover, Jesus said:

> *Ask,* and it shall be given you; *seek,* and ye shall find; *knock,* and it shall be opened unto you: For every one that asketh receiveth; and he that seeketh findeth; and to him that knocketh it shall be opened (Matt. 7:7, 8).

Jesus calls us to an approach wholly different from the natural human approach. The normal human approach is to start with ourselves as autonomous intellects and try to reason our way to God, the way we would investigate a scientific problem. But the true knowledge of God, though reason is involved as we have seen, does not yield to this method:

> O the depth of the riches both of the wisdom and knowledge of God! *how unsearchable are his judgments, and his ways past finding out!* (Rom. 11:33).

We can't find Him on our own — not by a bootstrap method. Jesus said we must start by *asking, seeking, knocking.* Newton would never have thought of *asking* gravity, a non-person, to lead him to discover its laws.

Asking implies an *interactive* process between persons; God is involved in your seeking. As we mentioned before, "God has His eye on you." Unlike gravity, He is sensitive to our seeking even before we ask. Without complicating this wonderful interactive process of knowing God, let it suffice for now that if we care enough to seek, God cares enough to *reveal Himself* and to *direct us* in our search. He is responsive enough to guarantee, according to His promise, that those who seek will find Him. That is why the advice of Jesus really works; in the end, God finds you!

Warming Up Toward God

Hardly could we be made in the image of God, created as rational, intelligent spirits, placed in an environment so carefully suited to our needs, and still not have a clue as to who we are or how we came to be. There are things about us that cannot be explained apart from God: like a universal sense of right and wrong, like the basic God-consciousness in all of us, like rationality and the ability to know, like thought itself that bubbles forth spontaneously; like love, humor, sorrow, and the burning questions about origins and destinies. We can readily see that we are wonderfully made. Isn't this alone reason enough to warm up a little toward God and try to hear what He is saying?

All these things suggest someone thoughtful has been at work on us before we ever began to think. Before Descartes said "I think, therefore I am," there was prologue. A rational work had been done long before, without which he never would have or could have said "I think."

These are some of the things Paul had in mind when he wrote, ". . . that which may be known of God is manifest in [us]; for God hath showed it unto [us]" (Rom. 1:19). Though this seems obvious, people by nature are not happy with it. By nature, Paul said, they try to suppress it. But even though we know we have sometimes done wrong, even against our *own* standards, it is useless to keep our guard up. God knows all about it.

Despite the human tendency to suppress this sense of God (Rom. 1:18), it keeps pressing itself upon us in innumerable ways. We find it recurring as an almost irresistible presupposition, and this should be accepted as a ray of hope — something we should encourage, not suppress.

There's no need to live in quiet frustration, avoiding the real truth. A few people try to resolve the tension by a bold, irrational, groundless decree that "there is no God" and retreat into atheism. Taking comfort in the "invisibility" of God, some say, like Russian Cosmonaut Yury Gagarin after the first space flight, "I saw no God out there."

Frank Borman, on the other hand, saw clearly the footprints of God from his orbit of the moon and read from Genesis to the watching world, "In the beginning God created the heaven and the earth. . . ." Only a few men have been as fortunate as Borman to view the handiwork of God from that vantage point, but we all have seen enough to understand God's eternal power. As we have previously discussed, "the invisible things of [God] . . . are clearly seen, being understood by the things that are made . . . ."

For this reason most people are unwilling to openly confess atheism. But it is a perplexing fact that many are content to practice it — to suppress their thoughts about God, to rationalize their behavior, or to trivialize God by merely patronizing His popular image as the doting old man "upstairs." Many go through life with a vague sense of God in the background, and they are careful to keep Him there. But all the subterfuge and rationalization, though they may temporarily allay fear of the real truth, finally leave us cold and alone with nagging "what if's." What if I must meet God some day?

It's time to soften up a little and begin to break the ice toward God. If He created us in His own image —

though we have marred that image — His thoughts toward us will not be all negative.

> For I know the thoughts that I think toward you, says the LORD, thoughts of peace, and not of evil, to give you a future and a hope (Jer. 29:11, NKJV).

God spoke these words to the captives in Babylon. Could it be very far from the thoughts He has toward you who seek Him?

What Kind of God?

Even after we admit we really should seek to know God, often human rationalization may continue. We want a *manageable* god; we sometimes retreat to a second line of rationalization and raise the question: But what kind of God? Rationalization of our obligations under God is treated in many ways. The most common way is to change the way we think of God into something that we can manage, control, or safely ignore. This has given rise to numerous kinds of gods throughout the history of the world. In discussing the tendency of humanity to suppress their consciousness of God, the Apostle Paul wrote:

> . . . when they knew God, they glorified him not as God, neither were thankful; but became vain in their imaginations, and their foolish heart was darkened. Professing themselves to be wise, they became fools, And changed the glory of the uncorruptible God into an image made like to corruptible man, and to birds, and to fourfooted beasts, and creeping things (Rom. 1:21-23).

Tough language! But we are not discussing a harmless, innocent problem. It is a self-destructive problem. It destroys lives both here and hereafter. It is essential then to answer the question: *What kind of God is God?*

If we are willing to eliminate the primitive and un-informed concepts of deity such as "fourfooted beasts," i.e., animal worship; sun, moon, and star worship; stock and stone idolatry; Greek mythology and the like, the alternatives are very few. Virtually all modern ideas of God with their many variations will reduce ultimately to three concepts: 1) *atheism,* no God; 2) *pantheism,* the belief that the universe or cosmos is God[1] (an imper-sonal Energy/Force/Oversoul); or 3) *monotheism,* a creating God – a personal, rational God.

The anxiety about meeting God, gnostiphobia as previously discussed, does not arise from atheism nor from pantheism. Those "gods" make no demands. If we can have *them* as our gods, the pressure is off, and humanity assumes personal autonomy as the highest intellect in the universe, answerable to no one! The dread and suppression arises from the sense that *the true and living God* is the transcendent, all-righteous, all-powerful, personal, communicating God of the Bible[2] under whom we are subordinate, morally accountable, and utterly dependent.

The Creating, Communicating God

If God is a rational, personal God, as we must con-clude, then we would expect Him to stand forth and *tell us plainly* who He is, what He has done, what His stan-dards of morality are, what He plans to do, and what He expects of us.

Now what a remarkable thing! We do find exactly that. The Bible claims to be, and in every way proves to be, God's verbal communication to mankind.

It could hardly be more direct and to the point. It reveals, from the very beginning of creation, that God has communicated with mankind, informing us of the origin of the universe and of ourselves, and has kept us informed of the progress of His purpose. And yet a large percentage of mankind is willfully ignorant of all this, and many view it with skepticism or a certain contempt.

If God is a *rational, compassionate* God, He must be a *communicating* God. He would lay the whole story before us in direct, understandable prose that would match up with the rational communications capabilities He designed into mankind. The Bible is the only holy book known to man exhibiting the dignity, merit and unassailable character of a comprehensive communication from God.

This book, centuries in the making, came not from an individual or committee. It has been thrust upon us by the almighty — *here!*

God will not quibble with us.

God resolutely enlightened us as His purpose unfolded, often before it happened. We did not ask for it; He proclaimed it.

He makes no attempt to "prove" it to us. If the heavens and the earth before us do not prove Him, what more could He say? "The heavens declare the glory of God; and the firmament showeth his handiwork" (Psa. 19:1-4).

The Bible's God is a unique God! No other holy book in the history of the earth independently presents a transcendent, rational, knowing, personal God.[3]

He is wholly different from the Eastern pantheistic god. The Eastern god is an abstract principle, not a transcendent Creator; that god is integral to and "evolving" with the universe; not a *person* who knows, operates, cares, and communicates. Atheism and pantheism are evolutionary by necessity, and the operative "creator" in them is *chance* — by definition a random, irrational, chaotic, phenomenon without intelligence, without order, without organization, without plan. We have seen already (chapter 1) how barren this theory is. God then is the hands-on Creator.[4]

The Transcendent God

We turn now to God's plain-language communication, where He reveals in lucid prose what kind of God He is. The opening statements of the Bible disclose extremely important truths which are amplified and confirmed throughout the rest of the Bible, as well as by the physical universe.

The God of the Bible is a *Transcendent* God:

• "In the beginning *God* . . ." (Gen. 1:1).

This simple phrase alone is sufficient to establish God's transcendency. Before anything else existed, He existed fully God. He was complete and self-sufficient *without* the universe, *before* the universe existed. The Eastern god, energy/force, requires physics, a universe, for being. God was in no way integrated into nor dependent upon physics or a universe for His being. He is supra-physical. We call that a *transcendent* God. God is a Spirit (John 4:24); the Bible represents God as a transcendent Spirit.

• "In the beginning God *created* . . ." (Gen. 1:1).

A transcendent God is fully capable of bringing the universe into being out of nothing, having the power of creation within Himself. Stephen Hawking describes a boundless universe and asks, "What place, then, for a creator?"[5] Little did he realize that he had just surrendered the only grounds he could ever have for rationality, for his ability to analyze and discuss the universe! Hawking cites no principle by which the leap may be made across the vast chasm from chance to rationality. What place, indeed, for a creator?

> Then answered the Lord . . . *Who is this that darkeneth counsel by words without knowledge? Gird up now thy loins like a man; for I will demand of thee,* and answer thou me (Job 38:1-3). . . . Wilt thou also disannul my judgment? wilt thou condemn me, that thou mayest be righteous? *Hast thou an arm like God? or canst thou thunder with a voice like him? Deck thyself now with majesty and excellency; and array thyself with glory and beauty.* . . . Then will I also confess unto thee that thine own right hand can save thee (Job 40:8-10, 14).

The nature of a transcendent God is that He is whole within Himself, the *first* cause. Therefore physicists, as well as others, are wholly dependent upon Him. That notwithstanding, many seem wholly oblivious to His eminent presence, not unlike the following scenario:

One morning, many years ago, I walked into my study to find a beautiful moth had been trapped between the window and the screen. It had fluttered hopelessly all night. Its wings were shredded, and its strength was fading rapidly. I spoke to it, "would you like to go free"? Then I cranked open the window and it fluttered out to freedom.

Apparently oblivious to the truth and reality of this situation, the moth went its way. Would it ever have believed, if it had been told, that a giant rational, person had seen its plight, that a surge of compassion had moved this giant person to speak to it, to release it, and to feel a wave of delight as the moth fluttered out to freedom? But if this had been told to the moth, it would have been *completely true!*

To compound the amazement, if the moth could have known, the rational powers and compassion of the person who opened the window was but the reflection of an infinitely greater transcendent person whose compassionate providence had actually superintended this entire event. This too was true, and we know it because, unlike the moth, we have been told!

This is not about emotion but objectivity. The wonder of this reality was probably lost on the moth, but it was not created with rational powers and is therefore blameless and may be excused. But naturalistic scientists and philosophers, oblivious to the giant Person who looks down with pity upon their arrogant efforts — while they generate endless theories to avoid recognition of Him who carefully provides for their thankless lives — these have been told and are hardly blameless. "For in him we live, and move, and have our being" (Acts 17:28).

Neither man nor moth is autonomous. As we flutter helplessly in our prisons of sin, beating our physical and mental "wings" to shreds on the way to the grave, we should humbly remember that our plight is under the conscious surveillance of God. We belong to Him body and soul. In light of this truth, there can be no independent human action, because the body by which we act is a prior work of God. There can be no independent human thought, reason, or conclusions; because the mind by which we reason is a prior work of God.

In the opening words of God's revelation, in less than a sentence, we are enlightened beyond all the "wisdom" and the speculations of godless philosophers of all time. In sublime simplicity, God imparts the most profound truth.

- "In the beginning God created *the heaven and the earth*" (Gen. 1:1).

This expresses the universality of God's work. All that we know as *universe,* all physical reality, all life, all psychic and rational phenomena are the works of God's creative power. There is no object, no principle of physics or life that does not hearken back to God for its being. *God is prologue to all things.* Therefore one cannot start with his own thought to reason his way to God or any other truth. If God is the God of the thought, the thought must presuppose His existence before it has any meaning. Before there was ever a thought, there was God.

A Personal God

The God of the Bible is a *Personal* God:

- "And *God said,* Let there be . . ." (Gen. 1:3).

We know who God is by what He has done. A God who *speaks* is a person, not an abstract, unconscious force or principle. A word, a thought, a plan, a rational deliberation, is a quality of *personhood* — everything that chance is not. The main characteristic of a person is self-conscious knowledge. A person perceives, understands, communicates; God considers, feels, empathizes, loves: "[God] found [Jacob] in a desert land, and in the waste howling wilderness; *he led him about, he instructed him, he kept him as the apple of his eye*" (Deut. 32:10).

God's personhood also responds negatively to negative phenomena. He has indignation and anger, but his indignation is always righteous. "God judgeth the righteous, and God is angry with the wicked every day" (Psa. 7:11). His righteous anger is kindled by rebelliousness, injustice, arrogance, lying, cruelty — namely, *sin.*

We can identify with God's compassion and His anger because we are persons; we are made in God's image. We understand a mother's love, a father's courage, a friend's loyalty. We know grief, joy, sadness, humor, anger, pleasure; these are not mysterious to us, for we are persons. But physics and chance are not persons; they cannot make persons. Evolution is not guided by a person,[6] thus persons did not evolve.

We have belabored the fact that God is a person so that we can easily grasp the idea. Actually, God is more — He is a Trinity, three persons in one. Not three Gods, but *one God* as three persons working in absolute perfect oneness and harmony. God has taught us to call these persons, the *Father,* the *Son,* and the *Holy Spirit.* This is a mystery, and there is nothing in human experience to which we can liken it; therefore we will not try to elaborate. Later we will see this aspect of God, especially the Son and the Holy Spirit, playing a prominent role in our salvation. God is a person. He knows you by name.

A Rational God

The God of the Bible is a *rational* God:

• "And *God saw* the light, that *it was good:* and *God divided* the light from the darkness" (Gen. 1:4).

God sees, thinks, evaluates, organizes, designs, and makes good. A God who works according to purpose, who reasons, organizes and makes useful, is a *rational* God. God created all *order* and *all physical, psychic, and rational phenomena, all thought processes and reasoning powers.* No man can possibly *know* except that a rational God had purposely designed and created him with rational faculties, with senses to detect the nature of his environment, with a mind to process information and communication and respond accordingly. Without this work of God, we could know nothing. Therefore, our very ability to think a reliable thought must presuppose a rational God. Without Him you could not be deciding about Him.

God's rationality includes knowledge, communication, love, goodness, order, beauty, consistency. *Chance* is chaotic, inconsistent, random, impersonal, irrational, blind, unknowing.

The God of the Bible is *transcendent, personal,* and *rational.* He knows, cares, communicates: "When Israel was a child, then *I loved him . . . I taught* Ephraim also to go, taking them by their arms; but they knew not that I healed them. I drew them with cords of a man, *with bands of love"* (Hosea 11:1-4).

In the Image of God

The God of the Bible created mankind in *His image:*

- "So God created man in his own image, *in the image of God created he him; male and female* created he them" (Gen. 1:27).

Since we are created in the image of God, the nature of man reflects certain of the characteristics of God. As God is a Spirit, man also is a spirit. After forming a body from the elements of the earth, God did something special; He imparted the spirit of life from Himself, "and man became a living *soul*" (Gen. 2:7). As already observed, a human is a *person;* unlike a stone or a tree, he or she has self-conscious awareness. As living persons, living spirits, men and women consciously and deliberately interact with their environment.

Moreover, men and women are *rational* persons. Their rationality involves intelligence, knowledge, logic, communications. We speak, send and receive communications both with God and our fellow persons. It seems inevitable that a *personal, rational* God would design the highest order of His creation to be *personal, rational* beings also.

As we reflect upon the final objective of God as related in the closing words of the Bible, it is a simple matter to conclude that an all-knowing, transcendent God would have designed His creation from the beginning to satisfy His ultimate goal:

> Behold, the tabernacle of God is with men, and *he will dwell with them,* and *they shall be his people,* and God himself shall be with them, and be their God (Rev. 21:3).

To achieve this ultimate union with mankind, God would need to communicate with us in this life, to reveal truth to us, for our own good. We would need to be able to receive God's communication and to respond to it. We would need senses to interface with our environment, the ability to process data and reach reliable conclusions.

More importantly, since God's plan for this union included the incarnation of Himself in man, as we will later see, it would be imperative that He would impart the aspects of His image that would foster a full and appropriate interface between the incarnate God and humanity. These are but a few ways in which *God designed us* to reflect His image and to interface rationally with Him.

So What?

Unfortunately, to make a case for the transcendent God does not always settle the matter. Even if the God of the Bible is the true God, some will still ask, so what? In reality this question is answered by the rest of this book, but briefly the point is this: Our lives, like it or not, are inevitably intertwined with God, and our present and eternal well-being requires that we acknowledge this reality. We are wholly *dependent* upon God for our personhood, rationality, life, and breath; therefore we must embrace a worldview that includes this truth or we will be eternal misfits in God's universe. We are utterly wrapped up in God — saturated throughout with His obvious being. "In him we live, and move, and have our being . . ." (Acts 17:28).

Every human mind that ever thought a valid thought has first been made, sustained, and influenced by the rational God. There is no autonomy; there is no independent or neutral thing or phenomenon in the universe that is unrelated to God — every fact, every object, every mind, every process answers to Him.

Therefore, a showdown, a day of reckoning is inevitable. "Wherefore . . . at the name of Jesus every knee should bow" (Phil. 2:9). The claim of autonomous man to be a personal, rational product of impersonal, irrational chance will be exposed. A person made in the image of God, cannot forever hide out in the fantasy-land of the naturalistic unbeliever without one day running headlong into reality with devastating consequences. The universe did not originate spontaneously, having no cause; this is a "flat-earth" mentality fostered not by ignorance but by a perverse arrogance. The universe is the work of a transcendent, personal, rational God. Our sense of God is real because He made it so. Both in our minds and in our hearts, we know this very well.

We have belabored this truth long and carefully. But for those who still resist and maintain their own autonomy or self sufficiency, the burden is upon them to validate, for themselves and others, their own grounds for rationality and the ability to *know* without reference to God.

But we trust there will be no resistance to God's great truths and that we may now turn together in confidence to God's verbal, objective revelation — the Bible.

The Problem of Insubordination

As we approach the question of sin, you who seek to know God can already sense the gravity of the matter, but you know too that there is a gracious solution. So we must press on through the tunnel toward the light with a healthy reverential awe.

The concept of insubordination raises the issue of authority, and to acknowledge a transcendent, personal, rational God is to acknowledge also His sovereign authority and our inherent subordination. Insubordination is disobedience to authority, i.e., the refusal of a person of inferior authority to submit to a person of superior authority. We may argue about authority figures among men, but if anyone would argue that God's ability to create galaxies, mice, and men out of nothing does not define an inherent position of superior authority then no other argument would suffice.

If the transcendency of God is not sufficient to establish His authority over all His creation, then further discussion is futile. If a human insists upon personal autonomy, or the authority of ultimate personal self-determination, this *ipso facto* places him on a collision course with God wherein the issue of ultimate authority must finally be resolved by power.

The God of the Bible *is* the ultimate authority. He *cannot* relinquish His authority, He *would not* relinquish it, and He *should not* relinquish it. *Authority* is intrinsic to *transcendency;* no created entity could possibly rise to the demands and implications of ultimate authority, ultimate knowledge, and ultimate power, all of which are inextricably bound up in God. Furthermore, any wish to have it otherwise is a death wish. This was the original sin and is at the base of all subsequent sins.

Adam and Eve were originally subordinate by nature. But that they might know this, agree with, and choose this position in conformity with the unchangeable reality of God's transcendent person, God conferred upon them the dignity of free moral agency. He did this by the introduction of a single minuscule inhibition. He forbade them the fruit of *one* tree!

Now those thoughtless enough to regard this biblical truth as a fairy tale unworthy of a Creator, or this inhibition as a trivial rule imposed by a petty deity, should pause long enough to think of what God accomplished by this act. He both honored them with the freedom of choice and devised, for their sake, an infallible test of insubordination or rebellion against authority.

To test for *insubordination alone,* the inhibition must be carefully chosen. It must not impose a burden of temptation in itself. It did not deprive them of food; there were *many* other trees for food. *The only effect was to draw a clear line of distinction between the authority of the Creator and the creature.* Although they were made in the image of God, there is still a vast difference, a boundary that cannot be crossed. The simple act of placing off limits a single tree, with others like it in abundance, placed no burden upon them except the burden of subordination. This act highlighted a very critical truth, the distinction between man and God in terms of authority and power, and achieved God's purpose with surgical precision.

This test was perfect; would they choose the truth, *subordination?* Or would they struggle for *equality,* or worse yet, superiority? Their choice was influenced by the intervention of another class of created being, a fallen angel, who had clearly chosen to attempt to gain *superiority.* His weapon was then, and continues to be, a lie. And Eve's first act of insubordination was believing the claim of a fellow creature that they would "be as gods." She tested the impassable boundaries of God's authority and power; she opted for insubordination, and Adam followed. They then had the knowledge of "good and evil" *experientially.*

A profound change took place in their character and in the character of all their offspring. That is why we today do not have to teach our children to be selfish, or to lie, or to fight, etc.; they do those things by nature. We carefully try to teach them the contrary, and still they do them! Thus, we all have an inherent depravity:

All humans, having a sense of right and wrong, now universally do wrong. "There is none righteous, no, not one . . ." (Rom. 3:10). And now, because of universal insubordination, there is an additional reason why we cannot find God by independent thought. We are now fallen creatures; we are damaged goods. We are all depraved by nature and utterly biased against God.

> And you hath he quickened, who were *dead in trespasses and sins:* Wherein in time past ye walked according to the course of this world, according to the prince of the power of the air, *the spirit that now worketh in the children of disobedience:* Among whom also we all had our conversation in times past *in the lusts of our flesh, fulfilling the desires of the flesh and of the mind; and were by nature the children of wrath,* even as others (Eph. 2:1-3).

This sinful orientation is at the root of human appetites for sin, of gnostiphobia, of suppression of the evidence of God, of stubborn disobedience, and willful ignorance of God's verbal communication, the Scripture. Apart from the input of God's Word and His Holy Spirit, we cannot and will not come to Him for light, despite our rationality. All this can be restored only by a work of God's grace.

Right and Wrong

The tree of the "knowledge of good and evil" is well named. Despite an inherited depravity, there remains in the whole human race an innate sense of good and evil, or right and wrong — with a strong propensity for wrong that cannot be satisfactorily explained apart from biblical creation and the Eden experience. There is a sense in all human beings, even within the most primitive tribes, that some things are right and some things are wrong. Not even postmodern pluralistic thinkers are exempt from this aspect of their humanity. They think it is *right* to think there is no right — nothing absolute.

The universal sense of right and wrong cannot be explained merely by what we have been taught. We may differ about what is right or wrong, but we all agree that there is *right* and there is *wrong*. Some have called it a sense of "ought" — a sense that some things *ought* to be and some things *ought not* to be.

As far back as the ancient book of Job, we find this sense operative, "If I justify myself," Job said, "mine own mouth shall condemn me: if I say, I am perfect, it shall also prove me perverse" (Job 9:20).

The Apostle Paul understood it well when he wrote:

> For when the Gentiles, which have not the law, do by nature the things contained in the law . . . . their conscience also bearing witness, and their thoughts the mean while accusing or else excusing one another (Rom. 2:14, 15).

For the conscience to "accuse or excuse" implies some sense of right and wrong, an appeal to some kind of built-in standard. Where did it come from?

The amoral neutrality of the naturalistic view of chance-origin could not account for it. That would imply that there is no right and wrong. It is rather a leap of blind faith to believe that the chance gyrations of randomly dancing molecules could universally and uniformly "conclude," in so many different heads, that there is a right and a wrong!

The great Christian writer and apologist, C. S. Lewis, was once an atheist. But he noticed that in every person there was a universal innate sense of right and wrong — even in an atheist's soul — that could not be explained apart from God. When Lewis later became a Christian, he wrote about this sense of right and wrong:

> . . . human beings, all over the earth, have this curious idea that they ought to behave in a certain way, and cannot really get rid if it[7]. . . . It looks, in fact, very much as if [they] had in mind some kind of Law or Rule of fair play or decent behavior or morality or whatever you like to call it, about which they really agreed.[8]

Growing out of this universal sense of right and wrong is the notion of justice. Even among the most liberal, no one believes that a person should have free reign to do anything whatsoever he chooses with no answerability or consequences at all. We all agree that there must be some standard of behavior to which we must answer — some set of consequences for violation of that standard of justice. Our laws and penal systems exist by the general consent that some things are wrong and ought to be punished.

If there had been no such sense in human nature, laws would never have been established or tolerated in human societies. The law of the jungle would be the norm.

Yet, the notion of justice is still ingrained in human thought by the influence of some great Reality. In extreme cases of wickedness the most calloused among us feel strongly that evil deeds deserve punishment. Millions were deeply incensed at the atrocities committed against the Jews by Hitler and his associates in World War II. These, and the myriad of lesser atrocities in history, have outraged the consciences of people all over the world. And even though we are plagued with a serious flaw in our perception of righteousness, as we shall later see, we sense that we do not live in a universe where cruelty finally wins. The innocent may not be brutalized by the cruel forever; the books of eternity will be balanced with justice someday!

This leaves us with an uneasy feeling, because we all have done things that by *our own standards* we know we ought not to have done and have not always done the things we know we ought. Despite our reluctance to acknowledge God, we sense that out there somewhere is a great universal Justice. Some prefer to think of it as an impersonal fate, but they have the feeling that "fate" has a way of evening the score — that there is ultimately a day of reckoning and that we will not finally get away with anything.

If our *own* standards of right and wrong in the secret chambers of the soul are more pure than our performance of them, how will we fare when measured by God's perfect, absolute standards? And because we believe in justice, we cannot avoid a certain anxiety that out there beyond the grave there awaits a great Supreme Judge who also believes in justice and will one day bring all things into balance.

When we say by our own laws and penal systems, that wrong ought to be brought to justice, we cannot make a very convincing case to ourselves that there is not a God of justice behind it all who says the same thing!

It poses then a problem of no small consequence to know in our hearts that there is right and wrong, that we have a strong propensity toward wrong, that wrong ought to be brought to justice, and yet we are not always sure what specifically is right and what is wrong. This raises the question of law. Since a transcendent God thinks of everything, we are not surprised to find that God in love has established *law.* "It was added because of transgressions" (Gal. 3:19), for at least two reasons: 1) To restrain sin and keep us from self destruction, and 2) so that we could know our sins and turn to the Savior for pardon, for by the law is the knowledge of sin (Rom. 3:19).

Therefore, in our quest to truly know God, we must now, in the next chapter, consider His law – "holy, just, and good." Even in the law, you who honestly seek the truth will see God's goodness and be directed by His law to the grace that is in Jesus Christ.

End Notes:

[1]The origin of the universe under atheism and pantheism is by necessity thought to be evolutionary. Pantheism, first implicit in the Vedic writings of the ancient Hindu bards, became the basis of virtually all the Eastern religions, the modern New Age movements, and is lately being integrated into modern scientific philosophies as the complexities of scientific discovery more and more require the acknowledgment of an intelligence behind the universe. The speculations of the Vedic writings as to origins are agnostic in tone differing little in that regard from that of the modern scientific philosophers. For example:

"That one thing, breathless, breathed by its own nature: apart from it was nothing whatsoever. . . . / Who verily knows and who can here declare it, whence it was born and whence came this creation? . . . / He, the first origin of this creation, whether he formed it all or did not form it, / Whose eye controls this world in highest heaven, he verily knows it, or perhaps he knows it not" (From *The Song of Creation,* in *The Rg-veda*).

Modern philosophers say that the center of a dialogue between religion and science " . . . would be a cosmos rippling with tension *evolving out of itself* endless examples of the awe and wonder of its seamlessly interconnected life. . . . a single significant whole." (Emphasis added). Menas Kafatos and Robert Nadeau, *The Conscious Universe* (New York: Springer-Verlag, 1990), pp. 187, 188.

[2]For an extensive discussion of the transcendent, sovereign, communicating God (the "talking God" as Carson puts it, p. 226), as traced in the "Bible's Plot-line," see D. A. Carson, *The Gagging of God* (Grand Rapids: Zondervan Publishing House, 1996), pp. 193-345.

[3]The Koran comes nearer than any, but the Islamic faith draws its concept of God from the Bible.

[4]There is no new god so far. In their attempts to derive a new epistemology from modern science, Kaftos and Nadeau admit, even in a book entitled *The Conscious Universe,* that *chance* remains the basis of evolution: "Mutations are *random* changes . . . resulting primarily from the *chance* bombardment of the master molecule by ultraviolet light from the sun, cosmic rays, nearby chemical reactions, and *random* quantum processes during reproduction" p. 94, (emphasis added). Furthermore, they essentially admit that their metaphysical theories of modern physics lead to the eastern religions like Hinduism, Taoism, and Buddhism, i.e., to pantheism (pp. 123-24), so what's new?

[5]Stephen W. Hawking, *A Brief History of Time* (New York: Bantam Books, 1988), p. 141.

[6]The theistic evolutionist would, of course, take exception to that claim. It is true enough that a transcendent, rational, personal God would be required to give the evolutionary process upward development against the Second Law of Thermodynamics, but here a serious dilemma develops:

1. The transcendent, rational, personal, communicating God is a God of righteousness, love, kindness, and benevolence.

2. Evolution is a process of cruel struggle, suffering, and death, wholly incompatible with the God of the Bible as a creation process, making Him self-contradictory. Theistic evolution as a theory is not self-consistent.

3. Moreover, the communicating God has denied evolution by His own verbal account of creation. This has serious implications; God is rational enough to speak His mind with exactitude and holy enough to speak with complete honesty. Where did He go so wrong in communication if evolution, after all, was His method of creation?

4. There are numerous theological contradictions in theistic evolution, not necessary to pursue here. It is more intellectually bankrupt than naturalistic evolutionary theories.

[7]C. S. Lewis, "The Case for Christianity," *The Best of C. S. Lewis* (Washington: Christianity Today, Inc., 1969), p. 405.

[8]Ibid., p. 401.

CHAPTER 3

The God Who
Loves and Legislates

We have considered briefly the very significant fact
that all people everywhere have become insubordinate
to God; and having a sense of right and wrong, they still
do wrong. But now we must consider *what specifically*
is right and what is wrong and the consequences of miss-
ing the mark. This brings us to consider a standard. It
is time to go beyond the vague built-in sense we all have
and find the objective standard detailing the specifics of
right and wrong.

This, in turn, brings us to consider *law.* Since the
Garden of Eden and the experience of insubordination,
human nature tends to bristle at the concept of law. But
it is just this characteristic that we must now face. Here
gnostiphobia reaches its peak, and here also is where
contemporary evangelists are weakest, doing their hear-
ers a great disservice. We must *know* our true standing
before the Supreme Judge; and if we are in jeopardy we
must seek the remedy before it's too late. Is there an ultimate standard? Is there penalty? Has God established a

law or does he merely offer some kindly optional advice?

This is where the "rubber meets the road," where our dread of the real truth often reaches its peak. If we are able to take to heart the truth about God's law and its penalty, the truth about His salvation and pardon (in the next chapter) will be a blessed relief. But if we take it lightly because of its discomfort level, God's offer of salvation will also seem a light thing.

Why Must We Consider Law?

If we are ever to have eternal life and be prepared to meet God, we *must* consider the basics of His law; but not for the reason you may think. The typical idea is this: "If I obey God's commandments pretty well and don't do anything really gross, then I'll go to heaven." Nothing could be further from the truth. However, God's righteous law does play a vital part in bringing us to salvation. This will become apparent as we go on.

But what do we mean by God's law? As used here, we mean *God's eternal, unchangeable principles of righteousness revealed in Scripture.* Some of God's commandments have been merely temporary expedients, to serve a temporary or symbolic purpose, e.g., animal sacrifice. Throughout the Bible, however, there are expressions of unchangeable principles of righteousness that God will *never* compromise. These are the eternal laws of God which we are discussing.

This study of law is not about what we *want* but about what is *true* and what we *need.* If what we want were doing the job, why is it that in the last decades of the 20th century the more people did as they pleased, the more gross and dangerous the moral character[1] of society became? The do-your-own-thing moral philosophy of the 1960's followed by postmodern pluralism has left its practitioners in great legal jeopardy before God. Yet legal jeopardy before God is not a class affair, but an individual affair. Every individual must answer to God.

The "Sermon on the Mount," among the most important of the teachings of Jesus Christ, is really about God's law. On that occasion He said:

> Think not that I am come to destroy the law, or the prophets: I am not come to destroy, but to fulfil. For verily I say unto you, Till heaven and earth pass, one jot or one tittle shall in no wise pass from the law, till all be fulfilled (Matt. 5:17, 18).

In that sermon, Jesus made a big issue of the matter of *motive* and *attitude* toward righteousness. He made it clear that the degree of righteousness God requires of us is greater than just a good score in the rote keeping of the law. In fact, the scribes and Pharisees had pretty high marks in that department; but Jesus said, ". . . except your righteousness shall exceed the righteousness of the scribes and Pharisees, ye shall in no case enter into the kingdom of heaven" (Matt. 5:20). We can sense already that Jesus is speaking of *a righteousness of quite a different order of magnitude and quality,* not just morally better, as we have previously observed, but finally perfect (Heb. 10:14). We will discuss this at greater length in a later chapter.

But it is important not to fall into the trap common to human nature: "If I'm really sincere and try really hard to do right — to keep the commandments, not take advantage of anyone, to serve others and not be a bigot or a hypocrite — then I think God will let me into His heaven." The God who created us to know the truth has revealed that nothing could be more futile. It seems obvious that a person who is insubordinate by nature and deed cannot get to heaven by any law or code of conduct which he has already broken. The Scripture declares it categorically: ". . . by the deeds of the law there shall no flesh be justified" (Rom. 3:20). Only one breach of the law disqualifies us from heaven in the first place. "For whosoever shall keep the whole law, and yet offend in one point, he is guilty of all" (James 2:10).

Then, you may be wondering, why on earth do we need to consider law? The answer, most germane to this discussion, is briefly expressed in the following explanation by the Apostle Paul:

> Wherefore the law is holy, and the commandment holy, and just, and good. Was then that which is good made death unto me? God forbid. But sin, *that it might appear sin,* working death in me by that which is good; *that sin by the commandment might become exceeding sinful* (Rom. 7:12, 13).

The principle expressed here is that the law reveals the "exceeding sinfulness" of sin. In addition to its intrinsic value, it is an objective yardstick by which to measure and recognize our deviation from God's perfect standard. The law is an instrument of condemnation only, not of pardon. Except for the condemnation of the law, pardon would be unnecessary. Condemnation is by law; pardon is by grace.

> "For by *grace* are ye saved through faith; and that not of yourselves: it is the gift of God: *Not of works, lest any man should boast*" (Eph. 2:8,9).

Grace, especially, distinguishes the Christian Gospel from all the other religions on earth. This truth will become abundantly clear when we have more fully considered the nature of the law, and it is virtually impossible to appreciate fully until we do.

One God, One Law

Since, as we have previously seen, all knowledge depends upon the reality that we are the creation of the rational, purposeful God of the Bible, we are endowed by our Creator with a faculty for rational discernment and a built-in sense of right and wrong. Thus we must look to Him also for the specific standard so that we can know what is right and what is wrong.

Any valid standard must find its foundation in the one absolute sovereign God.[2] We cannot find a supreme standard among men for two reasons: 1) We all are now by nature fallen, sinful persons, and 2) no person is supreme over another. There can be only *one* Supreme Being: "Hear, O Israel: The Lord our God is one Lord" (Deut. 6:4).

The "one Lord" is supreme. This is the foundational truth upon which all law must rest: there is *one* God. Law is law because it derives from an absolute. If there is *one* God, there is *one* law — one standard for right and wrong. Any law therefore, to have validity, must find its foundation in and be compatible with the *one* absolute law of the *one* absolute sovereign God.

In today's pluralistic society, as we have seen, the concept of objective truth has been all but abandoned. Truth for one person, they say, may not be truth for another. The moral standards of one person may not be right for another because, they say, every person has to decide what is *right for himself or herself.*

The validity of that philosophy depends entirely upon the kind of God that exists. As previously discussed, if *chance* is the creator not only is there no knowledge, there is no moral standard. The moral choice of one human is as authoritative as another, and we are back to the law of the jungle.

But we have seen that God is a transcendent, personal, rational God. A transcendent God is a God of sovereign authority. *We are therefore shut up to His moral authority as a standard for right and wrong.* What any person *thinks* is right and true *for himself or herself* has nothing to do with what is *actually* right and true. That is established by the *one* absolute sovereign God alone.

You may choose to believe in moral relativism, situation ethics, or that there is no objective truth, right, or wrong; but if you do, you surrender all standards and criteria for determining morality and ethics. Moreover, when you surrender these, all the great time-tested moral values evaporate. You are left naked, with nothing to wrap *your* "values" in but personal opinion. Furthermore, if you have nothing more than personal opinion to bring to the table of dialogue, the burden is upon you to show reason why you should be admitted to that table — or be heard at all.

We are back then to the *one* God, and all right and wrong must find its basis in His *one law*.

Now, since God is the one transcendent universal sovereign, *God's law is universal and timeless.* The principles of righteousness in God's law are universally and timelessly binding.[3] "I am the Lord, I change not" (Mal. 3:6). God's law is law for today. It was law last century and is law for the next millennium. It is law in America.

It is law in China and in Africa. It is law on Mars, on Jupiter, and in the constellation Andromeda. There is *one* God and *one* law.

What is Law?

What then is law? Suppose the legislative body of a state passed an act that read: "All citizens should refrain from stealing." Yet, there was no enforcement body established, and there was no penalty specified for its breach. Is this law?

Without *enforcement* such a "legislative" act would not be law at all. It would be only advice. *Law, then, is a rule or commandment enforced by penalty.* Without penalty it remains merely advice. Law is the establishment of statutes, principles, or rules by a bona fide authority having the power to enforce them by penalty.

A corollary of law is the concept of justice and the execution of penalty for the breach of law. The effect of law, and the well-being of the thing protected by the law, depends upon the application of penalty. Even human legislators typically make laws with high value and purpose, protecting the life, limb, or property of multitudes. These principles of law are considered by legislators, and citizens as well, to be of such value that they must finally be made to prevail above all who oppose them — by force if necessary.

Law is the only alternative to anarchy. We do not have to be theologians to understand this, for we can see it all around us in a lawless society. As the regard for the law of God diminishes, cruelty against the innocent, violence, debauchery, lewdness, and contempt for the person of others increase in direct proportion. Make no mistake; God will have no part of this. There is penalty attached to the breach of God's righteous principles and truths. He has established *law,* not *advice.*

With these consequences before us it is easy to see that law must be enforced by penalty. There is not a shadow of a possibility that the principles of God's righteous law will not finally be made to prevail throughout His universe. God's law, like God Himself, must finally be exonerated and vindicated because truth demands it; and truth will ultimately prevail, for God is truth. If God prevails, law must prevail. Thus law must carry a penalty.

Once we understand and accept the fact that God has given a law, that law carries a penalty, and that we are answerable to God for any breach of His law, we have taken a giant step toward finding peace with God. It may seem just the opposite, but we will never find peace with God while denying His law.

The Value of Law

How then should we understand the value, the infinite worth, of God's law? To really appreciate the goodness and beneficence of God in conferring His law upon us, we must realize that the quality of life we experience from day to day is a direct measure of the degree to which the law of God has influenced our social order. The difference between the Garden of Eden and a poverty stricken, crime ridden inner-city ghetto is obedience to God's principles of righteousness and truth. Implement the righteousness of the law throughout the earth, and the earth will turn into a virtual paradise. "And the Lord commanded us to do all these statutes, to fear the Lord our God, *for our good always, that he might preserve us alive . . .*" (Deut. 6:24).

We are taught both by nature and the Bible that *life* is good and therefore valuable. "And God saw every thing that he had made, and, behold, it was very good" (Gen. 1:31). Health is good, peace is good, economic prosperity is good; happiness, joy, kindness, courtesy, honesty, loving relationships — marriage, family, friendship, comradeship — all are good and therefore of great value and essential for life as God meant it to be.

All of these great values are preserved and promoted by the law — and experienced, to the extent God's law prevails in our society, to the inestimable benefit of all and the joy of the righteous.

Thus we see the value of His laws are infinitely high. The multitudes affected by them are innumerable. The benefit of God's laws to the obedient are inestimable. They are operative throughout vast ages and for all eternity. Toward this ultimate good all the purposes of God are finally moving, culminating in the "new heavens and a new earth, wherein dwelleth righteousness" (2 Pet. 3:13; Rev. 21:1-22:5).

The Trauma of Lawlessness

Consider now the contrary: the trauma produced by lawlessness. The breach of the law works death, disease, violence, poverty, anxiety, depression, cruelty, rudeness, lies, adversarial relationships, divorce, loneliness, enmity, hostilities. All lawbreakers inevitably experience one or more of these evils and often inflict them upon the innocent. *Lawlessness is at the root of all suffering, all pain, disease, agony, despair, grief, and the untold depths of sorrows in the composite experience of the whole human race.*

This composite suffering is the direct result of lawlessness or sin. Any breach of God's law by anyone at anytime therefore contributes to the composite suffering of humanity, which God's law was designed to prevent. Thus it is an attempted negation of God's wisdom and authority. It is an imposition of one's own wisdom and authority over that of God.

Though it may not always be the intent of the sinner, the breach of the law amounts to a vote for all the sorrows associated with lawlessness. It comes down on the side of suffering and death *against* peace and life. Every sin is an incremental contribution to all that we know as sorrow, pain and death. It is against all the good that God purposes to accomplish and establish throughout His universe. This reveals an irreconcilable difference in the attitude and character of those who stand on God's side in the matter of law and those who refuse to surrender fully to His authority and will.

Can God, therefore, ever come to terms with lawlessness? We may be assured that God will maintain His righteous law against all transgressors, enforcing it by penalty because of the great value of righteousness and the awful trauma of sin!

The Love in Law

Now we are prepared to see the *love* in *law.* Since this composite suffering is the direct result of lawlessness, it is inevitable that a God of love, in order to prevent such suffering, would maintain His law with all His power. Will a God of love abandon His people to lawlessness? *Will a God of love not hate sin, and its associated suffering, with an intensity equal to the love He has for righteousness with all its joy and glory?*

Somehow, in our generation, we have been conditioned to think of the enforcement of law with penalty as the opposite of love, when in reality it is one of the highest expressions of love. The classic 20th-century evangelical and fundamentalist theology (typified by Darby and Scofield) has painted God's law as a dark, onerous, loveless thing that has been discarded in this age. But this is grossly false. Jesus' understanding of the law includes not only *judgment* but *mercy, faith,* and the *love of God:*

> Woe unto you, scribes and Pharisees, hypocrites! for ye pay tithe of mint and anise and cummin, and have omitted *the weightier matters of the law, judgment, mercy, and faith.* . . (Matt. 23:23).

Then Luke adds to judgment, mercy, and faith, the love of God also:

> But woe unto you, Pharisees! for ye tithe mint and rue and all manner of herbs, and pass over *judgment* and *the love of God:* these ought ye to have done, and not to leave the other undone (Luke 11:42).

All these are "the weightier matters of the law." According to Jesus, the law involves mercy, faith, and love as well as judgment. Judgment is not incompatible with mercy and love. These are but different aspects of the interests, purposes, and love of God — to establish righteousness and blessedness for His own, eternally (Rev. 21; 22).

Because God is a God of love, He *must* punish wickedness which works against all the good that God purposes to accomplish and establish throughout His universe. So God's anger is directed against lawbreakers who abuse the objects of His love in behalf of those who love His righteousness:

> For the LORD your God is he that goeth with you, to *fight for you against your enemies, to save you* (Deut. 20:4).

> Then will the LORD be jealous for his land, and *pity his people* (Joel 2:18).

Then should we be surprised by the words of David who reciprocates this love toward his Lord:

> Do not I hate them, O LORD, that hate thee? and am not I grieved with those that rise up against thee? I hate them with *perfect hatred:* I count them mine enemies (Psa. 139:21, 22).

The Bible tells us that "God is love" (1 John 4:16), and we now can see that His wrath against sin is one major component of His love.

Sin — The Spirit of Lawlessness

It is the attitude of men and women toward the law of God that defines *sin:* ". . . sin is the transgression of the law" (1 John 3:4). More simply rendered: "sin is *lawlessness.*"

Sin is a lawless attitude that results in specific transgressions of the law (1 John 3:4). The persistent transgressor who continues to resist the restraints of God's law upon his behavior, who will not repent that he may be forgiven, who will not surrender his will and appetites to the control of his Creator, must finally experience the wrath of God.

The lawless *deeply resent the notion of an absolute law.* Human nature says, "Sure, I don't mind doing *some* of God's laws, but I will choose which ones. I will retain my own personal autonomy." That is lawlessness; that's God's definition of *sin* (1 John 3:4). The lawless would argue: "But I do not agree with the law; I have my *own* ideas of right and wrong and will do what *I think* is right for me."

If you chafe at the truth that God alone makes all the rules, is always right, always finally gets His way, then you have come upon the *very kernel of sin* — lawlessness. The unwillingness to agree and to surrender to God the full authority over yourself and His creation is the very epitome of sin.

In the final analysis sin is the attempt of the created to usurp the position of the Creator. The failure to obey and defend God's position against all others is rank insubordination which God calls *lawlessness.* "Nay but, O man, who art thou that repliest against God?" (Rom. 9:20). As we have seen, the Creator is always greater than the created, and when the created attempts or desires to reverse this — which is impossible — he has joined hard with the error of Satan who foolishly said: "I will exalt my throne above the stars of God . . . I will be like the most High" (Isa. 14:13). This is insubordination, lawlessness, *sin* in its grossest form.

The lawless also deeply resents being told what to do by another, by even God. The lawless insist on personal autonomy, self-determination, and self-indulgence.

Ordinarily people do not think of themselves as lawless; but if one is to be reconciled to God, that must change. How many principles of righteousness we have carelessly or deliberately violated, only God knows. All of us are guilty of breaking the "first and greatest" commandment:

> Thou shalt love the Lord thy God with all thy heart, and with all thy soul, and with all thy mind. This is the first and great commandment (Matt. 22:37, 28).

According to God's assessment, we all have been lawless; and without true repentance, we remain so. Everyone on this planet can pick one or more things out of the following list that they have done, or would have done if they could have:

> And even as *they did not like to retain God in their knowledge,* God gave them over to a debased mind, to do those things which are not fitting; being filled with all unrighteousness, sexual immorality, wickedness, covetousness, maliciousness; full of envy, murder, strife, deceit, evil-mindedness; they are whisperers, backbiters, haters of God, violent, proud, boasters, inventors of evil things, disobedient to parents, undiscerning, untrustworthy, unloving, unforgiving, unmerciful; *who knowing the righteous judgment of God, that those who practice such things are deserving of death, not only do the same, but approve of those who practice them* (Rom. 1:28-32 NKJV).

This is a partial listing of sins that violate God's absolute standards. But since the impenitent lawless *hate* the notion of absolutes, the universality and absoluteness of God's law is a prime target of the lawless, and the rejection of absoluteness in law is a rejection of the one God. This rejection is at best *polytheistic,* and at worst *atheistic,* because it presupposes many authorities or none at all.

But the lawless would rationalize: "I'm not lawless, I simply march to a different drummer."

But there is no other drummer. Don't you see? That is the issue. The lawless claim there can be another legitimate drummer — another standard. If you have some tendency to think this way or sympathize with this view, then you have discovered in yourself the very seed from which lawlessness springs. The unwillingness to let God be the most high — the final authority in all things — is *the* problem.

There is only *one drummer,* one standard, one God. But a lawless person disallows that — unless he or she is the drummer.

The Principle of Divine Retribution

Thus the line is drawn; the sinner has squared off against God: "the carnal mind is *enmity* against God: for *it is not subject to the law of God,* neither indeed can be" (Rom. 8:7).

This is war, and war must ultimately be resolved by *power.* God has the power, and we may be sure He will not surrender His universe to anyone, nor sacrifice His law on the altar of the personal autonomy of any created being. Until the sinner changes his mind and attitude, until he *repents,* there is an impasse. God offers pardon, but if the sinner will not yield by repentance, the impasse must be resolved by power.

Since this is war, and war is resolved only by surrender or by power, there are only three alternatives:

- God surrenders,

- You surrender, or

- It resolves to a power struggle; the most powerful one banishes the other to eternal isolation and retribution.

But God will win. The Creator by the nature of the case has all the rights, all the authority, all the power; in the end He gets His way every time! If you will not embrace this truth and rejoice in it, you must be His target. An eternal spirit in eternal rebellion must, of course, incur the judgment of God! Shall God sacrifice His universe and the glory of the world to come on the alter of the lawless? We all know the answer to that question.

For law to be law, there must exist a *penalty* and an *authority* having *power* to enforce it. God has the power; and He will, out of love for righteousness and the righteous, enforce the penalty. This leads us to the issue of divine retribution in the hereafter, or *hell*.

Although many people do not like to admit it, the conclusion now seems inevitable: There has to be a hell.

To clear up any remaining doubts, our communicating God has declared it. *Focusing the principle of divine retribution on the incorrigible, impenitent sinner is called hell.* Jesus described hell in the clearest possible terms (Luke 16:3; Mark 9:43-48; Matt. 8:12, 13:42, 50; Rev. 20:14,15). There is no ambiguity about the nature of hell. Jesus gave us graphic insight by His descriptions of hell. Consider, for example, the story of Lazarus and the rich man:

> ... the rich man also died, and was buried; And in hell he lift up his eyes, being in torments, and seeth Abraham afar off, and Lazarus in his bosom. And he cried and said, Father Abraham, have mercy on me, and send Lazarus, that he may dip the tip of his finger in water, and cool my tongue; for I am tormented in this flame. But Abraham said, Son, remember that thou in thy lifetime receivedst thy good things, and likewise Lazarus evil things: but now he is comforted, and thou art tormented.

> And beside all this, between us and you there is a great gulf fixed: so that they which would pass from hence to you cannot; neither can they pass to us, that would come from thence (Luke 16:22-26).

Jesus was able to communicate the truth as no other man. You can depend on the exactitude of His words, and though many may rationalize and play semantic games, His words could never mean anything short of a formidable sentence of divine punishment. The intensity of God's penalty for sin would be proportional to God's love for righteousness and for those who are the benefactors of His law.

What then is the purpose of punishment of the impenitent sinner? Although God's warning of such penalty may have some deterrent influence, penalty could not be for a deterrent purpose. If the sinner himself did not intrinsically deserve punishment, the potential of deterrence would not be an appropriate reason for penalty. A. H. Strong makes the observation: ". . . desert of punishment, and not the good effect that will follow it, must be the ground and reason why it is inflicted. The contrary theory would imply . . . that man might rightly commit crime if only he were willing to bear the penalty."[4]

Neither could final retribution be corrective, for Scripture teaches that after the final judgment there can be no correction for those who in eternal rebellion despise the mercy, goodness, and righteousness of God. "He that is unjust, let him be unjust still: and he which is filthy, let him be filthy still . . ." (Rev. 22:11). Correction cannot be retroactive.

Because contempt for a law more valuable than the lawbreaker is so heinous, the guilty inherently deserves penalty. This does not mean that a lawgiver enjoys the suffering of the lawbreaker, but that the alternative loss — of permitting the inherent value in the righteous principles of law to be lost, flaunted, or discredited — is so unbearable that the suffering of the less valuable lawbreaker is the only just alternative. Hence, "they which commit such things are worthy of death" (Rom. 1:32). Absolute maintenance of the law by penalty then becomes the just exoneration of law and of righteousness.

The punishment of evil is therefore inflicted 1) for the exoneration and vindication of the law, 2) because the lawless intrinsically deserve it, and 3) to restore forever the tranquility, peace, and joy of God's creation by the ultimate restraint and isolation of those forever committed to lawlessness.

The lawbreaker by negating the law is negating righteousness:

> "So long as God is holy, he must maintain the order of the world, and where this is destroyed, restore it. . . . the injury by which the sinner has destroyed the order of the world falls back upon himself — and this is penalty. *Sin is the negation of the law. Penalty is the negation of that negation, that is, the reestablishment of the law*" (A. H. Strong quoting J. H. Kurtz, emphasis added).[5]

It will not do to argue that God is too "good" to allow suffering. Visible examples are too numerous to recount. To the contrary, it is because God is good that He must punish sin which is the cause of all suffering. Consider the innocent child who is kidnapped, abused, or murdered by cruel and base men. The sense of justice in every normal thinking human being is outraged at these kinds of deeds. Even we ourselves establish punitive laws, after God, to deal with such offenders.

So, will not the Head of the universe balance the books of eternity with justice? Will He not avenge the suffering of the innocent while He vindicates and exonerates the righteousness of the law? God has told us in the plainest language that He will, and in our hearts we know it's true.

It is reasonable that the intensity and severity of the punishment will be in direct proportion to the intensity of God's love for righteousness. God's wrath blazes against those who would injure the objects of His love as intensely as His love burns for His own.

The anger of a mother is righteously directed against those who would abuse her baby, the object of her love, and we applaud her for it as noble and heroic. So is God's love when it blazes forth as anger in the care and protection of all that is right and good:

Thus God's divine wrath against sin is only the negative side of His love. They are inseparable. This generation must relearn that truth.

Lawlessness and the Conviction of Sin

One may consent intellectually to everything we have said so far, and still be at enmity with God. But now we come to the crux of the issue. Remember, we are spirits made in the image of God, and the Holy Spirit, the third person of the Trinity, is God's most direct interface with us.

It is the Holy Spirit, therefore, that turns the objective truth of God's Word and law into *inward persuasion or conviction.* He brings personal guilt for sin into sharp focus for the sinner. Then we stand convicted, guilty in our own eyes. Only then will a sinner repent and plead for mercy and the forgiveness of sin. Without this, there can be no forgiveness or salvation.

If you respond in humble contrition to the convicting Spirit of God, this is as close to God's wrath as you will ever come. If you resist Him and rationalize your guilt, this is only the "frying pan"; the fire comes in the hereafter. You must come to grips with the reality of your own personal sin just as all of us have done who have been forgiven and reconciled to God.

Sin is a word that has all but disappeared from the contemporary vocabulary. The world today, even many preachers, avoid it because they hate its connotations. We prefer to be victims: our behavior is a sickness, it's genetic, it's not our fault, we can't help it! But the word *sin* implies personal responsibility, moral obligation. It carries connotations of blame, reprimand, rebuke, censure, reproach, condemnation, reprobation. It means that at some point, somewhere, sometime, we have each taken a stand on the side of suffering and death against God's law; we are sinners. The Holy Spirit, as He applies the Bible's truth, takes away from us every vestige of self-righteous integrity and leaves us stripped and naked, wholly dependent on God's mercy:

As it is written, There is none righteous, no, not one: There is none that understandeth, there is none that seeketh after God. They are all gone out of the way, they are together become unprofitable; there is none that doeth good, no, not one. Their throat is an open sepulchre; with their tongues they have used deceit; the poison of asps is under their lips: Whose mouth is full of cursing and bitterness: Their feet are swift to shed blood: Destruction and misery are in their ways: And the way of peace have they not known: There is no fear of God before their eyes. Now we know that what things soever the law saith, it saith to them who are under the law: *that every mouth may be stopped, and all the world may become guilty before God* (Rom. 3:10-19).

No human being can lightly receive these implications, but this is God's view and the only accurate view of the natural human condition.

Because we are actually guilty, we must acknowledge our guilt before the law of God if we are ever to be reconciled with the God of truth and holiness.

To maintain that we are blameless before God's law adds dishonesty to the other breaches of the law and blocks any possible reconciliation with God. We have all at some time stood on the side of sin, death, and suffering against God, and until one repents and seeks God's forgiveness, he or she stands against Him still.

It is an elementary principle of biblical salvation that a sinner must stand *convicted* of sin in his own eyes before he could or would seek God's forgiveness through repentance. Such conviction is a work of the Holy Spirit: ". . . he will reprove the world of sin, and of righteousness, and of judgment" (John 16:8).

Those of us who have been there know that it is a heavy burden to acknowledge our just condemnation under the holy law of God; but when we appealed through repentance and faith to the sheer mercy of God and received His forgiveness, the contrast was glorious. As we confessed our breach of God's awesome law, and put our trust in Christ who "redeemed us from the curse of the law, being made a curse for us" (Gal. 3:13), the work was done; the heavy burden was lifted. So it will be with all who come to Christ by faith seeking forgiveness.

But who is this Christ that we might appeal to Him for mercy? What is this gracious work Christ has done to "redeem us from the curse of the law." Millions of people are as confused about who Jesus Christ is as they are about God and His law. But that need not be. In the next chapter we will unveil by the Scriptures the person who is the apex of God's redemptive love.

End Notes:

[1]The moral character of America remarkably declined in the last half of the twentieth century. Violent crime, premarital and extramarital sex, homosexuality, and immoral attitudes increased remarkably since 1960. Maybe Sodom and Gomorrah were a bit worse, but God destroyed them. The morals of Rome in its last days were closely parallel to those of the late twentieth century, and it was over-run by barbarians. What then is in store for us?

[2]R. J. Rushdoony, *The Institutes of Biblical Law* (The Presbyterian and Reformed Publishing Co., 1973) pp. 16, 17.

[3]This is not to deny that some of the laws given to Moses were temporary in nature, only because they were designed to serve a temporary purpose and had no intrinsic moral value. Most notable among these are the ceremonial laws of the Mosaic covenant — animal sacrifice and other symbolic laws that had their antitype in Christ and thus have completed their purpose. But throughout the Bible there are expressions involving unchangeable principles of righteousness that God will never compromise. These are the eternal laws of God which we are discussing.

[4]A. H. Strong, *Systematic Theology* (Valley Forge: The Judson Press, 1907), p. 655.

[5]Ibid., p. 660.

CHAPTER 4

The God Who Seeks and Saves

"Houston, we have a problem"!

Our studies in the first three chapters of this book have revealed a serious problem.

We have discovered that we were created in the image of a transcendent God, awesome in power, righteousness, and love; and this should be a reason for joy. We have discovered that God gave us a law that is holy, just, and good to preserve life, health, promote prosperity, and to keep us from grief and self-destruction; and this should be a reason for even greater joy.

Then why are we all not filled with delight? Simply because we all have been insubordinate to our transcendent Creator; we have transgressed His perfect law and incurred His righteous and just indignation. We have a problem.

It is unfortunate that along with the identity of the transcendent God we also uncovered a crucial problem. This, again, is where most contemporary evangelism is weak. It fails to reveal what it means to be at cross-purposes with a transcendent God — who is resolved that His universe will be filled with righteousness, life and health, peace and joy — no one would ever see the need to seek His forgiveness.

But thanks to His long-suffering, there is still opportunity and hope for those of us who are still living! God has made provision for our need, and it is our privilege now to examine His gracious solution.

God's Word to Man

The Bible, the remarkable number-one all-time best seller, has a central plot which is both a message and a person. It is a message in that it sets forth the solution for our need to be reconciled to God. But mainly, it is a person. God has provided a Redeemer to save us from the condemnation of our sin.

The central figure behind this plot or theme is introduced very early in the narrative. His message of hope runs through the Bible like a stream — getting wider and deeper as it goes until, like the mighty Amazon, it makes the final bend and glides into the placid ocean of God's eternal grace and glory. If you, like most people in this postmodern age, feel a little uncomfortable with this description, as if it were disingenuous, pretentious, or overstated — don't. If you ever really come to know God, you'll have to get used to some superlatives. It is impossible to fully state, let alone overstate, the grandeur of this Person and His redemptive work. In Him, God's *written* Word presents to us the *Living* Word:

> In the beginning was the Word, and the Word was with God, and the Word was God. . . . And the Word was made flesh, and dwelt among us, (and we beheld his glory, the glory as of the only begotten of the Father,) full of grace and truth (John 1:1, 14).

From the point of view of those who knew Him best, Peter says: "Whom having not seen, ye love; in whom, though now ye see him not, yet believing, ye rejoice with joy unspeakable and full of glory" (1 Pet. 1:8). Paul, as another benefactor of His grace, refers to the "peace of God, which passeth all understanding" (Phil. 4:7). And after discussing, in the book of Romans, many of the deep things of God, Paul spontaneously breaks into a lofty song of exaltation celebrating His wisdom, goodness, power, and glory:

> O the depth of the riches both of the wisdom and knowledge of God! how unsearchable are his judgments, and his ways past finding out! For who hath known the mind of the Lord? or who hath been his counsellor? . . . For of him, and through him, and to him, are all things: to whom be glory for ever. Amen (Rom. 11:33-36).

Those who know this Redeemer and have been reconciled to Him, though we have never seen Him, fully understand Paul's spontaneous paean of praise and can only add their heartfelt "amens."

From the Point of Need

The main plot was first introduced as God began His communication with His newly-created people very early, as soon as the need arose. We have previously considered the occasion, in the Garden of Eden, when Adam and Eve became insubordinate and incurred the just sentence of death and condemnation from the transcendent God. That was the point of first need. They needed hope and deliverance from the just condemnation upon their lawless insubordination.

This hope came in the form of a promise: A person, the *Seed* of the woman, would one day come to destroy the "serpent" who deceived them.

A dim hope, you say?

Though the narrative contains the barest description of the facts, Eve seized upon this promise with a tenacious faith. She had never borne nor even seen a child before, so naturally she would be amazed and thrilled — "I am wonderfully made," she doubtless thought, "I can bring forth persons from my own body"! When Cain and Abel came along, she probably thought one of them was the promised "Seed," and her faith burned warmly.

But then, from this pinnacle of joy, the course of events brought her to the depth of sorrow as she realized that the consequences of their insubordination were only beginning. Mystified and grief-stricken, she and Adam bent over Abel's cold, unresponsive body, and the magnitude of their problem began to dawn on them. They had never seen human death before. Is this what God had meant, "thou shalt surely die"?

At some point the initial realization of the gravity of their sentence came home to them: "Oh! Our children are affected — our beautiful children!" Their children had inherited their insubordinate attitude, their sinful nature, and their sentence of death; and their appreciation of the promise of the "Seed" took on very deep significance.

Then Seth was born, and we see Eve's faith in the promise bubbling up again as she proclaimed, "God has appointed *another seed* for me instead of Abel, whom Cain killed" (Gen. 4:25, NKJV).

Thus from the beginning of the human race, God provided a means of reconciliation through faith in a coming Redeemer. Though He would come late in history, the provision was made through faith in the promise that people from the beginning could be forgiven and reconciled to God if they would. Speaking of these early patriarchs, the writer of Hebrews observed:

> These all died *in faith*, not having received *the promises, but having seen them afar off, and were persuaded of them, and embraced them,* and confessed that they were strangers and pilgrims on the earth. . . . wherefore God is not ashamed to be called their God: for he hath prepared for them a city (Heb. 11:13, 16).

God's provision, in His own mind, began even *before* the problem arose. Knowing all things from before the beginning, God made provision for the salvation of mankind even before creation. Nothing takes a transcendent God by surprise, and so those who know Him are not surprised to read:

> Forasmuch as ye know that ye were not redeemed with corruptible things . . . But with the precious blood of Christ, as of a lamb without blemish and without spot: Who verily was foreordained *before the foundation of the world,* but was manifest in these last times for you, Who by him do believe in God, that raised him up from the dead (1 Pet. 1:18-21).

> [He was] the *Lamb slain from the foundation of the world* (Rev. 13:8).

God's provision is more than adequate for the salvation of all people from the beginning to the end. It is important that we understand that the unchangeable God has provided one and only one means of salvation.

All Nations Blessed

Several centuries after Adam and Eve's first encounter with death, God, pursuing His plan to bring a Redeemer into the world, repeated this promise to a man named Abraham. Although Abraham would be the father of a special people, Israel, this would be no mere tribal religion. He would be the father, spiritually speaking, of all men and women of faith throughout the earth (Gal. 3:9).

Long before the origin of Israel as a nation, God had already declared the blessings of redemption through the promised "Seed" to be *world-wide* in scope. He said to Abraham:

> And in thy *seed* shall *all the nations* of the earth be blessed (Gen. 22:18).

Abraham also, with a faith probably exceeding the faith of Eve, embraced the promises of God's blessings and the coming world-wide Redeemer; *"having seen them afar off,"* he was *"persuaded of them, and embraced them."*

Abraham, after these centuries, was well aware of the uniform depravity, sin, suffering, and death that now pervaded humanity. At God's instruction, he had moved away from the paganism and godlessness of his native land, and seeing the faithfulness of God, he fastened his faith upon the certainty and magnitude of His promises. Here we learn of God's remarkable and gracious response to Abraham's faith:

> And [Abraham] believed in the LORD; and *he counted it to him for righteousness* (Gen. 15:6).

From this it seems obvious that God's response to Abraham's faith was somehow very significant. But God would later give us even greater insight through the Apostle Paul and explain more fully the significance of Abraham's faith. Paul explained:

> For what saith the scripture? Abraham *believed* God, and *it was counted unto him for righteousness.* Now to him that worketh is the reward not reckoned of grace, but of debt. But to him that worketh not, but believeth on him that justifieth the ungodly, *his faith is counted for righteousness.* Even as David also describeth the blessedness of the man, unto whom God imputeth righteousness without works, Saying, *Blessed are they whose iniquities are forgiven, and whose sins are covered. Blessed is the man to whom the Lord will not impute sin* (Rom 4:3-8).

It is already becoming clear that sinners are justified by faith, not by good works. Faith is, and has ever been, the condition for salvation. The ancients *looked forward* to the coming Redeemer by faith in the promise, and God counted that faith as righteousness. But what about us?

> Now it was not written for his sake alone, that it was imputed to him; *But for us also, to whom it shall be imputed, if we believe on him that raised up Jesus our Lord* [the promised "Seed"] from the dead (Rom. 4:23, 24).

Now we see Jesus Christ as the one object of saving faith to people of all ages. They looked *forward* in faith to the promised Redeemer; we look *backward* in faith to the historical Redeemer with the same result. The result is that our faith is counted as righteousness. We become the recipients of a perfect standing before God, not in our own righteousness, but in the perfect imputed righteousness of God (Rom. 3:21, 22). Though He came late in history, He is the Savior to all peoples.

He will be a King

Leaving Abraham's day, we pass over many informative references and leap ahead several centuries to the time of David. The *kingship* of the coming Redeemer is so important that we must see how the promise of God was broadened with His promise to King David.

It is not possible for us to know all the reasons why God would single out certain individuals like Abraham, David, and others to make these great promises known; such things are buried in the complexity of God's sovereign purposes. "For who hath known the mind of the Lord?" Paul asks, "or who hath been his counsellor?" (Rom. 11:34). We know that David, like the rest of us, was a sinful man. God never hides such things; for the Bible, starkly honest even about its heroes, is quite explicit about David's sin. To say the least, it teaches us that God's grace extends to men with serious sins, and it can include us as well.

The Lord regarded David as "a man after [His] own heart." Perhaps it was the softness and godly sorrow of David's heart when confronted with his sin. David's sorrow for sin is obvious in his repentance:

> *Have mercy upon me, O God,* according to thy lovingkindness: according unto the multitude of thy tender mercies blot out my transgressions. Wash me thoroughly from mine iniquity, and cleanse me from my sin. *For I acknowledge my transgressions* (Psa. 51:1-3).

His faith in the grace and forgiveness of God was clear and complete. He wrote:

> The sacrifices of God are *a broken spirit: a broken and a contrite heart, O God, thou wilt not despise* (Psa. 51:17).

It is plain enough that the attitudes of humility, repentance, and faith — conditions which God demands of us all who would be forgiven of sin — were abundantly present in David. We should be instructed by this.

For these reasons possibly and for others that may never be known or for none at all, God conferred a special honor upon David in that the promised Seed would come through David's lineage. Moreover, in the latter years of David's life, God promised him that the Seed would be heir to "David's throne" and the dynasty of David would thus be established *forever:*

> And when thy days be fulfilled, and thou shalt sleep with thy fathers, I will *set up thy seed after thee,* which shall proceed out of thy bowels, and I will establish his kingdom. He shall build an house for my name, and *I will stablish the throne of his kingdom for ever* (2 Sam. 7:12, 13).

There are many grand implications in this promise, much weighty theology, which would be inappropriate to discuss here. But this much we should notice, that one who is able to occupy a throne *forever* is hardly to be regarded as a mere mortal like David or Solomon and his other descendants. This thought caught David's attention immediately, and he was struck with amazement, wondering is this merely a *human* matter?

> Then went king David in, and sat before the LORD, and he said, Who am I, O Lord GOD? and what is my house, that thou hast brought me hitherto? And this was yet a small thing in thy sight, O Lord GOD; but thou hast spoken also of thy servant's house for a great while to come. And *is this the manner of man,* O Lord GOD? (2 Sam. 7:18, 19).

We are getting glimpses, as the theme of God's revelation unfolds for us, that the promised Seed — while human for sure — is, well, *more* than human! David learned to refer to Him as the *Anointed* one or *Messiah* (see Psa. 2:2), and many other psalms refer to Him, including psalms about His suffering (Psa. 22) and about His kingship (Psa. 110).

Immanuel — God With Us

By the time David was old, he was fully persuaded that the coming *Messiah* (the anointed one, the *Christ*) would be somehow the incarnation of God in man. Although He would be David's "son" (i.e., grandson, many generations later) David called Him *Lord:*

> The LORD said unto *my Lord,* Sit thou at my right hand, until I make thine enemies thy footstool (Psa. 110:1).

So remarkable was this that the Messiah Himself would later call the attention of the unbelieving Pharisees of His day to this psalm of David to show that the Messiah was *more* than David's offspring:

> For David himself said by the Holy Ghost, The LORD said to my Lord, Sit thou on my right hand, till I make thine enemies thy footstool. *David therefore himself calleth him Lord;* and whence is he then [merely] his son? (Mark 12:36, 37).

As time went on God unfolded the main plot of the Bible more and more. It became quite apparent that the coming Seed, Redeemer, Messiah would be God incarnate, i.e., God enfleshed in man! And by the time of Isaiah, there was nothing left to ponder for it was categorically revealed:

> For unto us a child is born, unto us a son is given: and the government shall be upon his shoulder: and his name shall be called Wonderful, Counsellor, *The mighty God,*

The everlasting Father, The Prince of Peace. Of the increase of his government and peace there shall be no end, *upon the throne of David, and upon his kingdom,* to order it, and to establish it with judgment and with justice from henceforth *even for ever.* The zeal of the LORD of hosts will perform this (Isa. 9:6, 7).

This leaves nothing to doubt: *the Mighty God, the Everlasting Father,* was to be born into the human family as the second person of the Trinity, God the Son. Our transcendent God would condescend in mercy to become our Redeemer — as one of us!

"This is just too much," someone says. "You're straining my credulity."

But those of us who are fathers and mothers should not be surprised that a Creator would say to His people, "I created you, and you have sinned; but I will come to you and be your Redeemer." Would the bond of love of a Creator to His created ones be less strong than the natural bond He built into parents for their children? Yet, most normal parents would give their lives to save their children — even their wayward ones. Would God do less? "Yea," He said, "I have loved thee with an everlasting love: therefore with lovingkindness have I drawn thee."

But remember too, if one rejects the transcendent God and His own Word to us, he or she is back on *chance* — without credibility, passing judgments of the worst sort upon God!

These promises are *His* promises to us; we cannot sit in judgment of the transcendent God. With less than a century of experience, how presumptuous of one to say: "No, no, God cannot enter into and live in a human body. That is contrary to my experience; it cannot happen"!

A transcendent Creator, designing a human body

with the full knowledge that He would one day condescend to be our kinsman Redeemer and live for a time
in such a body, would certainly design that body to ac-
commodate His own Spirit. We are spirits made in His
image who live in bodies. Why then could not God, the
great Spirit, live in a body of His own design as He said?
This should in no way strain our credulity nor cast a
shadow on the credibility of God's communication to us.

No, this is a small thing if we believe in a transcendent God.

But back to Isaiah's day. God had offered to give
King Ahaz a sign of His faithfulness which Ahaz rather
self-righteously refused. But God said, well, He'd give
him a sign anyway. And the implications of the sign went
far beyond the problems of Ahaz's day. God said:

> Therefore the Lord himself shall give you a sign; Be-
> hold, *a virgin shall conceive, and bear a son, and shall
> call his name Immanuel* [i.e., God with us] (Isa. 7:14).

Then centuries later, God moved upon Matthew to
recall this promise and write of the birth of Jesus Christ:

> "Behold, a virgin shall be with child, and shall bring forth
> a son, and they shall call his name *Emmanuel,* which
> being interpreted is, *God with us*" (Matt. 1:23).

This is the theme, the plot, at the very heart of God's
communication; *God Himself would be our Savior.* There
can be no other.

Behold the Lamb of God

And now, we take the shoes off our feet for the
ground upon which we walk is holy ground. When you
understand this title, the Lamb of God, in your heart,

you are "nigh unto the kingdom."

The symbolic *lamb* entered the story-line of the Bible very early, at least as early as Abel when he offered "of the firstlings of his flock," and it was accepted by God.

The lamb was featured in the gripping story of God's test of Abraham's faith when he was to offer up his son Isaac as a sacrifice. We get a glimpse of the awesome message God was building into the symbology of the lamb when the boy Isaac asked his father the haunting question, "My father . . . where is the lamb for the burnt offering"? And we see the grasp of Abraham's faith in his calm reply, "My son, God will provide *himself* a lamb . . ." (Gen. 22:7, 8).

And then God made the lamb a central feature in the feast of the *Passover* which He instituted on the dreadful night when the death angel passed through Egypt taking the firstborn of those who defied God's commandment to let His people go. But He spared or "passed over" those who had faith enough to place the blood of the Passover lamb on their doorposts. Thus God established a great prophetic object lesson looking forward to the true Lamb of God to come.

Later, after the time of Moses, the concept of an innocent sacrifice substituted for the sins of the guilty would become central to the worship of Israel. During those centuries thousands of animal sacrifices were offered — until the lesson of a substitutionary atonement, the innocent for the guilty, was burned into the minds of God's people forever. By this graphic symbol the price in suffering, the blood, the life of the innocent necessary to atone for the sin of the guilty, was established beyond all equivocation. All this added fullness and unique meaning to the title *The Lamb of God.*

But all these references we had deliberately passed over until we came to the time of Isaiah. Here, Isaiah would be God's choice to most clearly open up for us the true meaning of this symbol as it would be applied to the coming Seed, the Redeemer, Immanuel — God with us, the *Lamb of God:*

> He was oppressed, and he was afflicted, yet he opened not his mouth: he is brought *as a lamb to the slaughter,* and as a sheep before her shearers is dumb, so he openeth not his mouth (Isa. 53:7).

Many centuries later, these haunting words would be read by a wealthy and powerful black man who was in charge of the treasury of Ethiopia. This man had the wisdom and humility to see his need and to seek the Lord's favor. He was reading the same verse quoted above, and like most people unfamiliar with the Scripture, had a little problem getting it together. He asked Philip the evangelist: "I pray thee, *of whom speaketh the prophet this? of himself, or of some other man?"*

This was a very good question. Is this a prophecy pertaining to the coming Redeemer, or does it refer to Isaiah or some unknown individual? We need to look into this matter more carefully. Would the one who was to be called "the mighty God" (Isa. 9:6) also be a sacrificial lamb? Was the incarnate (enfleshed) God to be a suffering Savior? Philip gave a very direct answer to the Ethiopian's question: "Then Philip opened his mouth, and began at the same scripture, and preached unto him *Jesus"* (Acts 8:34, 35). Philip had the advantage of hindsight since he lived after the coming of the Messiah.

But there is much more about this "man of sorrows" that we need to understand. A more detailed look at Isaiah's account will help us to see it all more clearly:

He is despised and rejected of men; *a man of sorrows, and acquainted with grief:* and we hid as it were our faces from him; he was despised, and we esteemed him not. Surely *he hath borne our griefs, and carried our sorrows:* yet we did esteem him stricken, smitten of God, and afflicted. But *he was wounded for our transgressions, he was bruised for our iniquities: the chastisement of our peace was upon him; and with his stripes we are healed.* All we like sheep have gone astray; we have turned every one to his own way; and *the LORD hath laid on him the iniquity of us all.* He was oppressed, and he was afflicted, yet he opened not his mouth: he is *brought as a lamb to the slaughter,* and as a sheep before her shearers is dumb, so he openeth not his mouth. He was taken from prison and from judgment: and who shall declare his generation? for *he was cut off out of the land of the living: for the transgression of my people was he stricken.* And he made his grave with the wicked, and with the rich in his death; because he had done no violence, neither was any deceit in his mouth. Yet it pleased the LORD to bruise him; he hath put him to grief: *when thou shalt make his soul an offering for sin, he shall see his seed, he shall prolong his days, and the pleasure of the LORD shall prosper in his hand. He shall see of the travail of his soul, and shall be satisfied: by his knowledge shall my righteous servant justify many; for he shall bear their iniquities.* Therefore will I divide him a portion with the great, and he shall divide the spoil with the strong; because *he hath poured out his soul unto death: and he was numbered with the transgressors; and he bare the sin of many, and made intercession for the transgressors* (Isa. 53:3-12).

This long passage gets to the heart of the main work

the Messiah has done to save His people from their sins. In this passage He is called simply "my righteous servant." The theme of a substitutionary sacrifice, the righteous suffering for the transgressions of the guilty, is the main feature of the passage: He has *borne our griefs and sorrows; He was wounded for our transgressions and iniquities, we are healed with his stripes.*

This is the message of all the sacrificial animals that had been offered through the years up to the death of Christ. Then God abruptly signaled the end of that system by rending the veil of the temple just as Christ, the true sacrifice, died on the cross (Matt. 27:51).

In the sacrifice of God's "Righteous Servant" a *satisfaction* was made. The Lord saw the "travail of his soul, and was *satisfied,*" for He would justify many by bearing their iniquities. How can we escape the conclusion that here God's Righteous Servant, the Seed of the woman, the Lamb of God, our Savior, is depicted as bearing the penalty for the sins of all who would receive it by repentance and faith?

But what was *satisfied* by the death of Christ? It would be left to the Apostle Paul to give the most concise explanation of the atoning work of Christ:

> Being justified freely by his grace through the redemption that is in Christ Jesus: Whom God hath set forth to be a *propitiation* through faith in his blood, to *declare his righteousness* for the remission of sins that are past, through the forbearance of God; To *declare,* I say, at this time his righteousness: *that he might be just, and the justifier* of him which believeth in Jesus (Rom. 3:24-26).

"Propitiation" is a legal term. In Isaiah 53:11, the Lord is said to have been *satisfied* by the sacrifice of His

Righteous Servant. In Romans 3:24, the meaning of propitiation must be essentially the same: to expiate, or to satisfy a legal requirement. It is clear enough from our study of the law, that we all are legally and justly condemned with the penalty of hell for our breach of God's law. But God in His love would pardon the penitent, forgive them, and spare them the just penalty of the law.

But could He?

Would He destroy the justice of His own righteous law by pardoning the guilty? Can a righteous judge refuse to enforce the penalty of law because the guilty party before him is family? If he does, some kind of legal satisfaction must be made.

When the interests of justice and the interests of love seem conflicted, we can appreciate the difficulty in finding a solution that preserves the interests of both. It is God's infinitely valuable and holy law that is broken, therefore only He can pardon and waive the penalty which He himself established. If God, however, would waive the penalty of law for a penitent sinner, the judicial responsibility to satisfy the penalty of law resolves back to Himself. He alone is responsible; He alone demands responsibility to Himself; and His suffering alone could satisfy His own system of justice and exonerate His law. To pardon the guilty, God must answer to His own system and sense of justice: "that he might be just and the justifier" of those who believe in Jesus.

God's atonement then is not a transaction with the sinner but with Himself! This is the hard reality of satisfying the interests of justice and love. Jesus, as the Lamb of God, resolved the impasse making our salvation just.

It is beginning to come clear. The Savior of a sinner condemned by law must be the *lawgiver,* God Himself. He must have also lived under the law as a man, and yet remained a *Righteous* Servant, wholly sinless and innocent. Moreover, He must be willing to exonerate the law He had not broken by bearing the just penalty due the pardoned sinner who did break the law.

Only One can qualify — the transcendent God incarnate in man, the Seed of the woman, the *Lamb of God.*

Identifying the Lamb of God

God sent a man whose main function in life was to officially identify this Savior when He came. John the Baptist one day stood on the banks of Jordan before a throng of people. Pointing to Jesus he cried: "Behold the Lamb of God, which taketh away the sin of the world" (John 1:29). The Lamb was here!

> . . . John seeth *Jesus* coming unto him, and saith, *Behold the Lamb of God,* which taketh away the sin of the world. . . . And John bare record, saying, I saw the Spirit descending from heaven like a dove, and it abode upon him. And I knew him not: but he that *sent me to baptize* with water, the same said unto me, Upon whom thou shalt see the Spirit descending, and remaining on him, the same is he which baptizeth with the Holy Ghost. *And I saw, and bare record that this is the Son of God* (John 1:29-34).

This was the official public introduction of the coming Messiah (the Christ) long awaited by Israel. Yet God did not leave this all-important identification — the climax of ages of prophecy — merely to the words of a man. Though John "bore witness" as God had told him, still God the Father Himself identified Jesus as the Messiah. When Jesus was baptized, the banks of Jordan were thronged with thousands of people who had come from Jerusalem to John's baptism. Then God spoke from heaven:

> And Jesus, when he was baptized, went up straightway out of the water: and, lo, the heavens were opened unto him, and he saw the *Spirit of God descending like a dove, and lighting upon him: And lo a voice from heaven, saying, This is my beloved Son, in whom I am well pleased* (Matt. 3:16, 17).

Thus with this miraculous manifestation of the Holy Trinity before all the people, Jesus of Nazareth was announced to be the Son of God by the Father Himself. Perhaps no other event in the history of the world has been better attested and authenticated than the advent of the Lamb of God that takes away the sin of the world.

It is true that even before this official identification, several individuals close to the family knew that Jesus was the Messiah. Elizabeth, the mother of John the Baptist, and Mary, the mother of Jesus, were cousins. They had spent three months together when they were respectively pregnant with John and Jesus thirty years before the Jordan event. They marveled that they had been chosen to this honor; they rejoiced together, they sang, they exulted, they praised the God of heaven.

This was no secret among their humble neighbors of the Judean hill country where Elizabeth and her husband Zechariah lived. There was among them a sense of awe mingled with hope, wanting to rejoice and shout but thinking, as humans do, "what if it isn't what it seems to be"?

> And fear came on all that dwelt round about them: and all these sayings were noised abroad throughout all the hill country of Judaea. And all they that heard them laid them

up in their hearts, saying, What manner of child shall this be! (Luke 1:65, 66).

Then when John was born, Zechariah, filled to overflowing by the Holy Spirit, broke his silence and explained to his neighbors and to the world the true meaning of these wonders:

> Blessed be the Lord God of Israel; for *he hath visited and redeemed his people,* And hath raised up an horn of salvation for us in the house of his servant David; *As he spake by the mouth of his holy prophets, which have been since the world began* . . . To perform the mercy *promised to our fathers,* and to remember his holy covenant; The oath which he sware to our father Abraham . . . And thou, child, shalt be called the prophet of the Highest: for thou shalt *go before the face of the Lord to prepare his ways;* To give knowledge of salvation unto his people by the remission of their sins, Through the tender mercy of our God; whereby *the dayspring from on high hath visited us,* To give light to them that sit in darkness and in the shadow of death, to guide our feet into the way of peace (Luke 1:68-79).

Zechariah, knowing that John would go before the Lord "to prepare his ways," boldly proclaimed that God had "visited" His people. All the promises we have reviewed were not wasted on Zechariah, who knew them well. He recognized exactly what was going on, that the "dayspring," the Lord from on high, had *visited us,* bringing light to we who sit in darkness and in the shadow of death.

To Confirm the Promises

Six months later, an angelic host from heaven visited certain shepherds in the hills of Judea and announced the birth of the Savior. The shepherds hurried to Bethlehem and worshipped Him who was the

Seed of the woman, a virgin. He had arrived as God had promised. The transcendent God now, mysteriously, was incarnate in human flesh!

Thirty years later, John the Baptist would make the official announcement, "Behold the Lamb of God," from the banks of Jordan. There Jesus of Nazareth would begin the short public ministry, just over three years, that would have the most profound effect on the world of any event in history. If He was the incarnate God, we could expect no less.

But what would He do?

He would begin with the greatest of all needs; as Zechariah said, "To give light to them that sit in darkness and in the shadow of death." This He did. His first priority was to bring light and truth to set people free from the captivity of sin:

> The Spirit of the Lord is upon me, because he hath anointed me to *preach the gospel to the poor;* he hath sent me to *heal the brokenhearted, to preach deliverance to the captives,* and recovering of sight to the blind, *to set at liberty them that are bruised,* To preach the acceptable year of the Lord (Luke 4:18, 19).

This is still His mission through the church He left behind.

But also, He would be concerned that people make the connection between all the promises God had made throughout the Bible and their actual fulfillment. We must know that Jesus of Nazareth was the Seed, the Messiah, the Mighty God, the Lamb of God who came to take away "the sin of the world," and our sins in particular if we seek Him.

He must "confirm" the promises, demonstrate them

to be true. If He is the transcendent God, what He does must show it. If we are to trust that He can pardon sin, save us from death and hell, provide an eternal home in heaven, then our faith must rest on genuine evidence (Heb. 11:1) that the promises and the fulfillment are one seamless piece of truth. God was concerned that we *know* that Jesus was who He claimed to be; He did the things that would confirm His identity.

Thus Jesus would do the things that only God can do and thereby validate the promises made long ago. Paul explained:

> Now I say that Jesus Christ was a minister of the circumcision for the truth of God, *to confirm the promises made unto the fathers* (Rom. 15:8).

And this He did: In bringing the good news of His saving Gospel, no other man "spoke like this man." In doing the supernatural works that only God can do, no other man even comes close. No Guru in history is in the same class; not Buddha, not Mohammed, not Confucius, not the Dalai Lama.

Jesus would set right the things that are wrong:

Blindness is an unnatural problem; Jesus healed the blind.

Lameness is contrary to God's original creation; Jesus healed the lame.

Death is an impostor in God's perfect creation; Jesus raised the dead.

He stilled the storms of the sea. He fed five thousand with a few loaves and fishes. He walked on water. He is Lord of nature, Lord of economics, Lord of disease, Lord of governments, Lord of life, Lord of death, Lord of time and eternity. He is my Lord, and yours.

What He did is sufficient to stop every mouth.

He did what God would do in a world wracked with sin. *His miracles were small-scale demonstrations of His power ultimately to restore all things completely to the perfection that existed before sin entered.* When He comes again the second time, He will *"make all things new"* including a new heaven and a new earth (Rev. 21, 22).

For over three years He busied Himself proclaiming the truth of salvation, making things right, doing good. But at the end He turned his attention to the fulfillment of the most dreadful promise of all — to become the true Lamb of God.

The Final Hours

As the earthly ministry of Jesus Christ drew to a close, the reality of human insubordination that originated in the Garden of Eden was drawing to its logical conclusion. The point has already been made, in the last chapter, that lawlessness ultimately resolves to war, i.e., to a test of force or power. It is wholly predictable that the presence of God among men would result in a violent use of force against Him. A little over three years is all it took until insubordinate humanity, true to character, squared off against the incarnate God to take Him out by force.

Jesus, who knew the Scriptures in all its profundity, fully understood the work He had come to do. He was not yet ready to meet the lawlessness of man with a show of power; that must await His second advent some time in the future. For now His role as the Lamb of God must occupy His full attention.

How often had He reviewed Isaiah 53? "He is despised and rejected of men; a man of sorrows, and acquainted with grief: and we hid as it were our faces from him; he was despised, and we esteemed him not" (v.3). How true it all had proved to be!

Lawless people, until seriously challenged, seem nice enough; but when faced with the unflinching consistency of God's righteousness, how soon the mask changes its visage.

On Tuesday of that final week, Jesus had His last interface with the leaders. He described lawlessness the way it is, mincing no words (Matt. 23); from that time they would not rest until they had apprehended Him.

We have emphasized that He was God, but He was also fully man. A heaviness came over His soul, and He retreated in the final hours to the garden of Gethsemane to pray.

"Now My soul is troubled," He said, "and what shall I say? 'Father, save Me from this hour'? But for this purpose I came to this hour" (John 12:27). Fully aware of what He must do, the Righteous Servant was about to actualize the role of the Lamb of God. Who can doubt that Isaiah's words rang in His mind:

> But he was wounded for our transgressions, he was bruised for our iniquities: the chastisement of our peace was upon him; and with his stripes we are healed (Isa. 53:5).

But could there be another way? "O my Father," He prayed, "if it is possible, let this cup pass from Me: nevertheless not as I will, but as you will." Yes, there was a way to avoid this ordeal:

> Or do you think that I cannot now pray to my Father, and

he will provide Me with more than twelve legions of angels? *But how then shall the scriptures be fulfilled, that thus it must be?* (Matt. 26:53, 54).

He *could* have saved Himself; but if He saved Himself, He could not save you or me. There was no way to do both; so He opted, praise His name, for us!

They came for Him with swords and spears; insubordination had now led to its inevitable conclusion, a war with God. But He was not ready yet to meet force with force; that awaits another day. Yet no one took His life from Him, "I lay it down," He said, "of myself."

It is Finished

Passing over the injustice of His "trial," we find a mixed crowd, about nine o'clock in the morning, milling around three crosses on a hill. Some few were there because they knew what was happening; they knew the story-line of the Bible, and felt the least they could do was to be there.

But most were there because their leaders were there to see that this troublesome man was once and for all silenced.

They seemed unusually bold and self-assured. They taunted, "if thou be the Son of God, come down from the cross." The chief priests and the scribes mocked Him, "He saved others; himself he cannot save." Little did they realize what profound truth they had uttered.

But about noon, the mood began to change. The crowd could sense that something unusual was happening. Then the noonday sun grew dim, a murky darkness settled across the land, and the brassy notes of arrogance were muted. Somber, uneasy tones of doubt and uncertainty droned throughout the nervous crowd.

On this scene God the Father would frown in His displeasure, as if to warn the forces of darkness of a day yet to come when every knee would bow and every tongue confess that the One upon the cross is Lord — when the organ of eternal justice shall echo throughout the halls of perdition with the thunder of God's final judgment for the impenitent and lawless — when the very angels of God hide themselves and there is silence in heaven until the Lord of hosts is exalted in judgment, and the Holy God is sanctified in righteousness.

For three hours the heavens were black. Darkness blanketed the land. But His mission was ever before Him: "Father, forgive them," He cried, "for they know not what they do."

In this dark hour, alone, alone, the Lamb of God absorbed the bitter verdict for sin and satisfied the legal demands of His own perfect law. "Thou shalt make his soul an offering for sin . . . He shall see of the travail of his soul, and shall be satisfied: by his knowledge shall my righteous servant justify many; for he shall bear their iniquities."

Finally the silence was broken by a bewildering cry, "My God, my God, why hast thou forsaken me?"

What went on at that moment within the Holy Trinity? Wisdom will not dare to answer and humility will not dare intrude. This is the Holy of Holies where only the High Priest enters! We can only look on with awe and boundless gratitude that the transcendent God is a God of love and mercy — not of justice only.

Again the silence was broken with the words, *"It is finished."* When Christ died, the promise which God had kept before His people of the Lamb of God as one "slain from the foundation of the world," that long prologue was finally complete. It was finished.

Late in the afternoon Jesus was given a hasty burial, but three days later on the first day of the week He arose from death, "because it was not possible that he should be held by it" (Acts 2:24).

He appeared to His disciples numerous times, confirming to them still that He was the transcendent God. Then He ascended before their eyes into heaven where He will reign "till he hath put all enemies under his feet" (1 Cor. 15:25).

Seeking and Saving

It should be apparent by now that the transcendent God is a God of "manifold grace" (1 Pet. 4:10). He creates, communicates, loves, legislates, seeks, saves, and so much more.

> O LORD, how manifold are thy works! in wisdom hast thou made them all: the earth is full of thy riches (Psa. 104:24).

From the moment Adam and Eve hid from God, He came seeking them. "Then the Lord God called to Adam . . . 'Where are you?'"

In the broader sense, all of God's works which we have discussed above are only the manifestations of His purpose to "seek and to save that which was lost" (Luke 19:10).

> This is a faithful saying, and worthy of all acceptation, that *Christ Jesus came into the world to save sinners;* of whom I am chief (1 Tim. 1:15).

But a few questions now remain: How does He save those who are lost? How does He interface with us who are sinners? What does He expect of us? How must we respond? What is it like in terms of human experience to be reconciled to God? What will be the results of it; and how will we know when we are saved, forgiven, the penalty lifted, and if we will go to heaven when we die?

We will examine these questions in the final chapter.

CHAPTER 5

Knowing God in Experience

We have examined at some length the character of God as our transcendent Creator, our serious status as sinners before His righteous law, and His relentless labors in bringing Christ into the world as the Lamb of God. We have considered the death of Christ on the cross for our sins, His resurrection from the dead and ascension into heaven. These are objective, historical works of God; and now we raise the issue, what do they mean in your experience?

Now, it is clear enough that our status in eternity will turn upon our attitudes toward these great truths and events. The attitudes of men and women toward events of such magnitude will be the focus of God's attention when He sits upon the great white throne to balance the scales of justice in the universe.

It is disturbing that most of the world today seems to be saying "So what?" This blind and mindless response can only add insult to the guilt of lawlessness. This response will never be acceptable to God.

In contrast, acceptable attitudes are exemplified by the great servants of the Lord throughout the Bible:

When Paul recognized the risen Christ he fell on his knees and said, "Lord, what wilt thou have me to do"?

Job, when confronted by God, said, "I abhor myself, and repent in dust and ashes."

David cried out:

> Wash me thoroughly from mine iniquity, and *cleanse me from my sin. For I acknowledge my transgressions:* and my sin is ever before me. . . . For thou desirest not sacrifice; else would I give it: thou delightest not in burnt offering. The sacrifices of God are *a broken spirit: a broken and a contrite heart,* O God, thou wilt not despise.

These men made the connection between the God of mercy and their sinfulness. They were brokenhearted over sin, and God forgave them and gave peace and salvation to them all. Business as usual was not an option in their minds. When they heard the good news of God's mercy extended toward the guilty, their minds were changed at once, that is, they repented and appealed to the Savior in faith for forgiveness. This is the only way of salvation.

Save, Saved, Salvation

These words are very important words that God has used numerous times throughout the Scriptures. The word *saved* appears about fifty-seven times in the New Testament alone. In all but about half dozen cases, it refers to the supernatural work of God in rescuing a sinner from the condemnation of sin and from eternity in hell. It is a word used to express that special work of God whereby He instantaneously and permanently pardons a penitent individual from the condemnation of sin and preserves him or her ever after for eternity in heaven. *Save, saved, salvation* are but different word forms referring to the same thing.

Sometimes people are uncomfortable using these words or hearing them because of their serious implications, but we trust we have by now left gnostiphobia far behind us. God's words best convey God's message. For example He says:

> Look unto me, and be ye *saved,* all the ends of the earth: for I am God, and there is none else (Isa. 45:22).

> Neither is there *salvation* in any other: for there is none other name under heaven given among men, whereby we must be *saved* (Acts 4:12).

> How shall we escape, if we neglect so great *salvation* . . . ? (Heb. 2:3).

> For by grace are ye *saved* through faith; and that not of yourselves: it is the gift of God: Not of works, lest any man should boast (Eph. 2:8, 9).

Each individual must make the connection between God's objective, historical works to provide *salvation* and our personal need of His *salvation.*

After coming this far in pursuit of truth, if it still seems abstract and impersonal, something is seriously wrong. We must remember, it was essential for God Himself to originate, initiate, and implement His redemptive plan. These are historical events that were accomplished by God Himself. Even before we were born He took the initiative and made these broad objective preparations. But *salvation* itself is very personal. Don't misunderstand, we do not save ourselves. But God saves individuals, specifically, who respond to Jesus Christ and

His offer of salvation through repentance and faith.

The application of God's redemption is focused and very particular to the individual. God has saved individuals all along the way since the beginning, and so today He continues to seek and save sinners. But it is always one by one, name by name.

Salvation is not attained by class action — not by a group, church, or movement one can join. God singles us out; the issues are drawn between God and you — God and me.

"Be Ye Reconciled to God"

When enmity exists between two parties, there will be no peace until each one is reconciled toward the other. Reconciliation, however, normally begins with a conciliatory gesture on the part of one party. God through the broad conciliatory work of Jesus Christ on the cross has initiated the reconciliation process. He has reached out toward sinners:

> *Now all things are of God,* who has reconciled us to Himself by Jesus Christ . . . that is, that *God was in Christ, reconciling the world to himself,* not imputing their trespasses to them . . . (2 Cor. 5:18,19, NKJV).

This conciliatory work was done by Jesus Christ on the cross in making legal satisfaction for sin under the requirements of His law. No greater gesture toward reconciliation could be made.

Moreover God's work toward reconciliation continues through His people as ambassadors. We who are reconciled to Him are to deliver this message calling other individual sinners, person by person, to reconciliation:

... and [He] has committed to *us* the word of reconciliation. Now then, we are ambassadors for Christ, *as though God were pleading through us:* we implore you in Christ's behalf, *be reconciled to God* (2 Cor. 5:18-20, NKJV).

Now, we have previously seen that we were all guilty before the law and were thus at enmity with God. Where there is enmity between two parties, even if one party is conciliatory toward the other, there is still no bonding unless the other is responsive. It takes two to be fully reconciled. When a breach occurs in human affairs between peers very often both parties are to blame, and in such a case reconciliation would require both to admit their wrong and seek the forgiveness of the other.

But in the case with God and man, mutual apology as peers is not at all in view. God is the lawgiver. He has done no wrong and has no blame. Man is fully to blame. Although God has graciously settled all the legal requirements necessary to forgive sin, He will not ignore a disposition or attitude of continuing pride, blame-shifting, excuse-making, self-righteousness, and insubordination. God requires humility, contrition of heart, and an honest admission of sin in repentance and faith. Reconciliation to God must be according to truth. We are the ones who are wrong.

I acknowledged my sin unto thee, and *mine iniquity have I not hid.* I said, I will *confess my transgressions unto the LORD;* and thou forgavest the iniquity of my sin (Psa. 32:5).

If we confess our sins, he is faithful and just to *forgive us our sins, and to cleanse us from all unrighteousness* (1 John 1:9).

God made *conciliatory* gestures of the most selfless

kind. Now the finger of guilt points to us. We are obligated to stand forth immediately before God in humility and honesty and confess, "I have sinned. I am to blame. I repent, forgive me."

Apart from this, there can be no reconciliation with God, and you must meet Him one day as your enemy. But if you can find a softness in your heart toward God and will repent and put your trust in Him to save you, He will forgive you, cleanse, and keep you, and reserve for you a home with Him in heaven.

Repentance and Faith

But perhaps we should take a deeper look at repentance and faith in case there is still some confusion about it. Before Jesus went away He made clear what He expected of us:

> And said unto them, Thus it is written, and thus it behooved Christ to suffer, and to rise from the dead the third day: And *that repentance and remission of sins* should be preached in his name among all nations, beginning at Jerusalem (Luke 24:46, 47).

All God's works, from the Garden of Eden forward, were done that all who would repent and look to Christ in faith for forgiveness of their sins could be pardoned and receive the free gift of eternal life. Jesus said it was *necessary* for Him to suffer and rise from the dead that *repentance and forgiveness of sin* should be preached everywhere.

God has placed the obligation of repentance and faith upon us all. There is not a shadow of a possibility that an exception will be made. Those of us who preach, or write the good news of salvation are required, as Jesus said, to preach repentance. If the necessity for repentance is not central, along with faith, to the evangelistic message, it is not a biblical message. We learn this from the biblical evangelistic preachers:

- **John the Baptist:** *"Repent ye:* for the kingdom of heaven is at hand" (Matt. 3:2).

- **Jesus:** *"... repent ye, and believe the gospel"* (Mark 1:15).

- **Peter:** *Repent ye* therefore, and be converted, that your sins may be blotted out (Acts 3:19).

- **Paul:** ... Testifying both to the Jews, and also to the Greeks, *repentance toward God, and faith toward our Lord Jesus Christ* (Acts 20:20, 21).

This emphasis on repentance and faith is uniform in the Bible. Repentance is a deep-seated change of mind — from lawlessness to full subordination — out of a godly sorrow. Faith involves an implicit trust, and more. Both are inseparable graces essential to salvation, and where one is stated the other is always implied.

The requirements of repentance and faith are not arbitrary; they are essential elements of reconciliation toward God. Without repentance you remain lawless, insubordinate, and hard-hearted. Without faith you hold God to be untrustworthy, calling Him a liar (1 John 5:10). This is not reconciliation. The sovereign God will not allow a person into His heaven unless these attitudes are changed.

Repentance and faith are inseparable. You can't have one without the other. They are *non-meritorious* graces wrought by the Holy Spirit. Many people confuse these with meritorious deeds or good works. But salvation is by *grace*, the *undeserved* or *unmerited* favor of God, *through* repentance and faith. The Bible presents them as *essential* to salvation by *grace:*

> Therefore *it is of faith, that it might be by grace;* to the end the promise might be sure to all the seed (Rom. 4:16).

In contrast, works are presented as unacceptable, and incompatible with grace, as a *condition* of salvation:

> And if by *grace,* then is it no more of *works:* otherwise grace is no more grace. But if it be of *works,* then is it no more *grace:* otherwise work is no more work (Rom. 11:6).

Moreover, unless we seek salvation through faith, it cannot be by grace. As we have seen, "it is of *faith,* that it might be by *grace"* (Rom. 4:16). We are told also:

> But Israel, which followed after the law of righteousness, hath not attained to the law of righteousness. Wherefore? *Because they sought it not by faith, but as it were by the works of the law* (Rom. 9:31, 32).

If we offer to God "good" deeds as meritorious toward salvation, then such "salvation," if it were possible, would not be by *grace.*

Repentance and faith are case-essential for salvation by grace, and a sovereign requirement of God. We do not negotiate with Him. God in His sovereignty could have elected to send every sinner into hell — repentance or not — and would have been perfectly just in doing so. But He didn't; in mercy He offers salvation by sovereign grace.

Because God is right and we are wrong, it is our *solemn duty* to repent, and to do it immediately. Even if God had not promised salvation, it would still be the duty of every sinner to repent — to change his mind about God and sin — because it is right. Yet, in mercy He promised. He made a bona fide offer of grace to those who repent of their sins and appeal to Him in faith for mercy.

> The Lord is not slack concerning his *promise,* as some men count slackness; but is longsuffering to us-ward, not willing that any should perish, but that *all should come to repentance* (2 Pet. 3:9).

The response of repentance and faith is the only *conciliatory* response a human can make to the long prologue of God's work on our behalf. This work includes His creation, all His works which we have reviewed above, His communications, His providential care, His Gospel and atonement for sin on the cross, His continuing appeal through His people, the direct and intimate drawing of His Holy Spirit in conviction of sin through the law and in revealing His goodness through the Gospel. If you remain impenitent and unmoved by all this, God will not accept you into His heaven.

Conviction of Sin

Salvation is of the Lord. It is not an accurate notion, though many people have it, that one may play the field, procrastinate, and think that any time they so desire they'll just make a "decision" and repent. If you are unmoved today by God's goodness, and you can trample His grace underfoot today, how will tomorrow be different? A godly sorrow works repentance to salvation (2 Cor. 7:10). Will you be sorry tomorrow but not today? There's more to this matter than a mere "decision."

The attitude and response God seeks is one of

faith and repentance out of a godly sorrow for sin:

> But *without faith it is impossible to please him:* for he that cometh to God must believe that he is, and that he is a rewarder of them that diligently seek him (Heb. 11:6).

> For *godly sorrow worketh repentance to salvation* not to be repented of: but the sorrow of the world worketh death (2 Cor. 7:10).

> Or despisest thou the riches of his goodness and forbearance and longsuffering; not knowing that *the goodness of God leadeth thee to repentance?* (Rom. 2:4).

The attitude God is seeking is a soft and tender heart, broken about sin, with a humility that acknowledges sin and the need for forgiveness:

> *The sacrifices of God are a broken spirit: a broken and a contrite heart, O God, thou wilt not despise* (Psa. 51:16, 17).

It is possible for one person to tell another that a heart broken over sin with a broken and contrite spirit is necessary for repentance, but one person cannot tell another *how to have* a broken and *contrite spirit* or a *"godly sorrow."* Neither can you switch sorrow on and off at your pleasure.

A sinner "dead in trespasses and sins" has nothing within, of himself or herself, to produce a godly sorrow for sin. Some *other* influence must be at work in your life. The only influence that can do this is the Holy Spirit. Only He can persuade or convict you of your guilt before the law or of the "goodness of God" through the Gospel and produce within you a "godly sorrow" that you might repent.

It is not in our power to simply make an independent "decision." If your thought is to "enjoy" your sins until late in life or even until tomorrow and then to repent, you are on dangerous ground. A death-bed repentance is not impossible, that none may despair; but it is highly improbable, that none may presume.

Then what can you do? Jesus said, "Seek and you will find." This is His promise. He will respond to your sincere plea for help, and you will find conviction, a godly sorrow, and true repentance and faith.

Only when we stand convicted of sin in our own eyes through the work of the Holy Spirit can we repent, and that is an awesome experience. But it drives us to Christ for forgiveness and salvation. This is no abstraction; it is an *experience*. We do not mean a mystical, subjective experience out of your own self. Salvation is an objective work of God toward you and within you; He pardons, justifies, and assures you in response to sincere repentance and faith, and you *experience* the peace it brings.

David described his experience in very graphic terms:

> *The sorrows of death compassed me, and the pains of hell got hold upon me: I found trouble and sorrow. Then called I upon the name of the Lord; O Lord, I beseech thee, deliver my soul. Gracious is the Lord, and righteous; yea, our God is merciful* (Psa. 116:3-5).

Though this may be a more graphic description than some people experience, the main elements of David's experience are present in *every* genuine case of salvation. When we acknowledge in our private heart our guilt before God's law and the just penalty of hell, that's "trouble and sorrow." Then to call upon the Lord out of that sorrow is virtually spontaneous, *"O Lord, I beseech thee, deliver my soul!"* Out of your anguish, you trust your case fully to Christ, seeking His forgiveness and His salvation. He then forgives, saves, and relieves your distress. More concisely:

- You are convicted of sin and deeply distressed.

- In repentance and faith you cry to the Lord for mercy and forgiveness.

- He forgives, saves, assures, and relieves your distress.

True to His promise, He forgives you, cleanses you, and makes of you a new person and receives you to himself as a son or daughter, saved, and directly procured for heaven. The Holy Spirit imparts a sense of acceptance, of assurance, of family:

> For ye have not received the spirit of bondage again to fear; but ye have received the *Spirit of adoption, whereby we cry, Abba, Father. The Spirit itself beareth witness with our spirit, that we are the children of God* (Rom. 8:15, 16).

The same Holy Spirit who *convicted* us of sin, now *assures* us of acceptance into the family of God. The Spirit who brought "trouble and sorrow" now brings "joy unspeakable and full of glory." This is a new birth, regeneration, an objective work of God (John 1:13) in the heart, but *we realize it as an experience.* Jesus explained the experiential aspect of it as follows:

> The wind blows where it wishes, and *you hear the sound of it,* but cannot tell where it comes from and where it goes. *So is everyone who is born of the Spirit* (John 3:8 NKJV).

Doesn't it make sense that if a person is drowning,

he calls out for help, and someone throws him a lifeline and pulls him to safety that he would know the difference between the terror of drowning and the joy of safety? When you are saved, God takes away the terror and replaces it with gratitude and a reverential awe of His love, mercy, and power.

When you are saved, God wants you to know it. You would be of little value as an ambassador, if you were always malingering in the shadows of doubt. Thus He assures us:

> Verily, verily, I say unto you, He that heareth my word, and believeth on him that sent me, *hath everlasting life, and shall not come into condemnation;* but is passed from death unto life (John 5:24).

> My sheep hear my voice, and I know them, and they follow me: And *I give unto them eternal life; and they shall never perish,* neither shall any man pluck them out of my hand (John 10:27, 28).

> . . . for *I know whom I have believed, and am persuaded that he is able to keep that which I have committed unto him* against that day (2 Tim. 1:12).

God's work of salvation is perfect. He who promised will deliver His people, every one, safely into His presence to spend eternity:

> And I heard a great voice out of heaven saying, Behold, *the tabernacle of God is with men, and he will dwell with them, and they shall be his people,* and God himself shall be with them, and be their God. And God shall wipe away all tears from their eyes; and *there shall be no more death, neither sorrow, nor crying, neither shall there be any more pain:* for the former things are passed away (Rev. 21:3, 4).

This is our final destiny with the Lord in heaven. This is the target that God was aiming at before the foundation of the world. God always hits His target. You can *know* where you will go when you die.

We have gone with you as far as we can go. The rest is between you and the Lord. All that is left to do, if you haven't already, is for you to petition Him for the forgiveness of sin and keep your case before Him until you receive satisfaction and the assurance of salvation:

> *Seek ye the LORD* while he may be found, *call ye upon him* while he is near. Let the wicked forsake his way, and the unrighteous man his thoughts: and let him return unto the LORD, and *he will have mercy upon him;* and to our God, for *he will abundantly pardon* (Isa. 55:6, 7).

The Fruits of Salvation

After you have come to know Christ as your Lord and Savior, as we have discussed above, your new life with God is just beginning. As we noted early in this book, the objective of God through Christ is not just to give us longer life but eternal life, not merely to be re-formed but born again, not merely to be morally better but ultimately perfect in the hereafter.

The eternal life God gives is characterized not only by its duration but its quality. In duration it is everlasting, and in quality the ultimate objective is a state of sinless Christ-likeness.

To look at our new life in yet a different way, we may compare our *judicial standing* before God with our *actual behavior* before Him. We have discussed briefly the matter of our *justification* by faith whereby God declares the believer to be justified, forgiven, and wholly righteous in His sight. This is our judicial standing in God's sight; we stand in the perfect righteousness of Christ:

> Even *the righteousness of God which is by faith of Jesus Christ* unto all and upon all them that believe: for there is no difference (Rom. 3:22).

This is not our behavioral righteousness but an *imputed* righteousness:

> But to him that worketh not, but believeth on him that justifieth the ungodly, *his faith is counted for righteousness.* Even as David also describeth the blessedness of the man, *unto whom God imputeth righteousness without works,* Saying, Blessed are they whose iniquities are forgiven, and whose sins are covered. Blessed is the man *to whom the Lord will not impute sin* (Rom. 4:5-8).

This describes our *standing in grace* before God the instant we repent and believe in Jesus Christ. This standing is eternal and guarantees our acceptance into God's heaven. It is judicially *imputed* or *counted* to the believer's credit based upon Christ's full atonement for all our sins when He died on the cross. This standing is wholly by grace. What a perfect salvation; how can we help but love Him!

But now, what about our actual behavioral state before God? It is far from righteous. We came to Him for forgiveness and cleansing with all the hang-ups of the former life, wearing the grave-clothes of sin and depravity, with all the very motions and habits of sin. And God graciously and *instantaneously* gave us a perfect and permanent standing. But at that instant the *habits* of the former life were still with us, ingrained in the gray matter and neurons of our bodies. *But now we are to begin the life-long process of bringing our personal behav-*

ior into harmony with our perfect standing. We are now
to rehabituate and bear the fruits of our salvation in righteous behavior. This is not in order to go to heaven, for
that is settled by grace. Righteous behavior is not the
cause but the *effect* of salvation. It is a serious but very
common error to get this order reversed; it reverses
the object of our faith from faith in Christ to faith in ourselves and reveals a fatal misunderstanding in the entire nature of salvation.

When God gave us a perfect standing, He also per-
formed another wonder. He changed us inside, permanently:

> Therefore if any man be in Christ, he is a *new creature:*
> old things are passed away; behold, all things are become
> new (2 Cor 5:17).

In the new birth, God has imparted to us something
of His own nature so that there is a fundamental change
toward godliness. It has not yet destroyed our "old"
appetites and attitudes, but it gives us new, godly, appetites and attitudes. This "new man," as Paul calls it,
motivates and enables us to grow and bear the fruits of
salvation in righteous behavior. Colossians 3:5-14 and
Ephesians 4:22-32 are classic passages on this process.

This growth follows the pattern of "putting off" the
sinful habits of the old life and "putting on" the godly
behavior of the new life. This process neither saves us
nor keeps us saved; we have seen, salvation is by grace.
But the growth process throughout life demonstrates
that we are saved. "Wherefore by their fruits ye shall
know them" (Matt. 7:20). A person who professes to be
a Christian but does not show the pattern of growth in
personal righteousness outlined in Scripture, must be

concerned. Was his or her profession genuine? Was he or she deceived in some way? Or is he or she merely a hypocrite? Genuine salvation bears fruit toward godliness.

The initial stages of fruit-bearing or growth in righteousness as commanded and exemplified in Scripture is to identify with Christ and the institutions He established to aid us in our growth. First, we are to identify with Christ Himself. We openly confess Him as our Lord and Savior. We confess Him both with our mouths, verbally, and with our lives.

The initial act of obedience which identifies us with the name of the holy Trinity — Father, Son, and Holy Spirit — is baptism. It also identifies us with the church Christ established which, among other things, assists us in our growth in godliness:

> Then they that gladly *received his word were baptized:* and the same day there were *added unto them* [the church] about three thousand souls. And they *continued stedfastly in the apostles' doctrine* and fellowship, and in breaking of bread, and in prayers (Acts 2:41, 42).

This is the biblical Christian norm. Find a church that carefully follows the Scriptures. Be baptized, learn and serve in truth — the "apostles doctrine," in fellowship, communion, and prayers. Any lifestyle that does not include these basic things is in no way compatible with the Christian profession.

If we do these things, we will honor our Lord and be blessed by Him, both now and for eternity.